WILD & WACKY

TRIVIA

717 Brain Drainers

that'll Stump Ya!

13-Digit ISBN: 978-1-60433-339-8
10-Digit ISBN: 1-60433-339-1

This book may be ordered by mail from the publisher. Please include $4.95 for postage and handling. Please support your local bookseller first!

Books published by Cider Mill Press Book Publishers are available at special discounts for bulk purchases in the United States by corporations, institutions, and other organizations. For more information, please contact the publisher.

Applesauce Press is an imprint of
Cider Mill Press Book Publishers
"Where good books are ready for press"
12 Port Farm Road
Kennebunkport, Maine 04046

Visit us on the Web!
www.cidermillpress.com

Design by Tilly Grassa, TGCreative Services
Illustrations courtesy of Anthony Owsley
Cover design by Whitney Cookman

Printed in China

1 2 3 4 5 6 7 8 9 0
First Edition

CONTENTS

Big Screen/Little Screen

1) **Edith Head has won eight Oscars. What was her job in movies?**

a) **Costume designer**   b) **Cinematographer**

c) **Director**   d) **Screenwriter**

****

2) **Julie Andrews won a Best Actress Oscar for the first movie she was in. What was the movie?**

3) Match the sports movie to the sport.

a) *Rudy*
b) *Miracle*
c) *The Bad News Bears*
d) *Chariots of Fire*
e) *Breaking Away*
f) *Rocky*
g) *Hoosiers*

1) Bicycle racing
2) Track
3) Football
4) Basketball
5) Hockey
6) Baseball
7) Boxing

4) **Did Shia LaBeouf make the first Transformers movie before or after he played Mutt in *Indiana Jones and the Kingdom of the Crystal Skull*?**

5) Who played Carol Ferris in The Green Lantern?

* *

6) WHAT OTHER SUPERHERO MOVIES, BESIDES *SUPERMAN RETURNS*, DID BRYAN SINGER DIRECT?

I THOUGHT I WAS GETTING TOP BILLING IN THIS MOVIE!

A) *X-MEN* AND *X2*

B) *SPIDER-MAN 2* AND *SPIDER-MAN 3*

C) *THE GREEN HORNET*

D) NONE OF THE ABOVE

7) What is the name of the girl who plays on the Mighty Ducks team in all three films?
a) Carol   b) Connie   c) Catherine   d) Cynthia

8) True or false: Justin Timberlake was the voice of Boo Boo in the movie *Yogi Bear*.

9) True or false: There's a movie called *Phffft!*

10) True or false: There's a movie called *Santa Claus Conquers the Martians?*

11) Complete the titles of these films, which are all part of the National Film Registry.
a) *How the West Was* _____ b) *The Bridge on the* ____ *Kwai*
c) *Easy* _____ d) *The Ten* _____

12) **Complete the titles of these films, which are all part of the National Film Registry.**
a) *A Streetcar Named* _____
b) *Raiders of the Lost* _____
c) *Night of the Living* _____
d) *Gunga* ____

13) **What was the first name of the first *Blue's Clues* host?**

14) Which Wiggle (or, at least, what color shirt Wiggle) left the band because of an illness?

15) True or first: One of the most popular kids' TV shows of the 1950s featured a puppet named *Howdy Doody.*

16) Were there more episodes made of *Happy Days* or *Laverne and Shirley*?

17) WERE THERE MORE EPISODES MADE OF *THE COSBY SHOW* OR *X-FILES?*

18) Were there more episodes made of *Charmed* or *Bewitched?*

19) Were there more episodes made of *Will & Grace* or *I Love Lucy?*

20) Were there more episodes made of *Star Trek: Voyager* or *Star Trek: Deep Space Nine?*

21) True or false: England had a children's TV series called *Mr. Noseybonk.*

22) True or false: In Italy, a popular children's show was *Geppeppippeppipep's Garage.*

23) True or false: One of the most popular children's shows in Latin America in the late 1980s was *Xou da Xuxa.*

24) True or false: There was once a TV show called *My Cave and Welcome to It.*

25) True or false: There was once a TV show called *My Mother the Car.*

WIPE YOUR FEET BEFORE COMING IN!

26) True or false: There was once a TV show called *The Ken Berry Wow Show.*

27) What does GSN stand for?

28) WHAT LANGUAGE IS TELEMUNDO BROADCAST IN?

29) What does OWN stand for?

Protoplasmic Life Network

30) What did AMC originally stand for?

31) What does IFC stand for?

32) What does CMT stand for?

33) Which network focuses primarily on the arts?
 a) RFD-TV   b) Ovation   c) ION   d) Halogen

34) What used to be the name of Nick Jr.?
a) Nothin' b) Noggin c) Nudge d) Origin

35) True or false: SyFy used to be Sci-Fi.

36) True or false: NBC Sports
Network used to be called Versus.

37) What network shares
channels with Cartoon Network?

38) True or false: TruTV used to be Court TV.

39) WHAT DID THE vH IN vH1 ORIGINALLY
STAND FOR?

40) True or false: There was once
a TV show called *The Hangman of
Hesher Hollow.*

41) True or false: **There was once a TV show called *Pink Lady and Jeff*.**

42) True or false: There was once a TV show called *Dundee and the Culhane*.

43) True or false: There was once a TV show called *Jake and the Fatman*.

· ·

44) What is the name of the famous singer who made her movie debut in *Funny Girl?*

· ·

45) Jennifer Hudson won Best Supporting Actress for her first movie. What was the name of it?

46) Justin Henry was the youngest actor ever nominated for an Oscar. How old was he in *Kramer vs. Kramer?*

47) True or false: A film critic named David Manning, quoted in ads for *A Knight's Tale, The Animal,* and other movies, was made up by the Sony marketing department.

● ●

48) What is the last name of Shia LaBeouf's character in the Transformers movies?

    a) Whitiker   b) Witwicky

    c) Wochovsky   d) Wallenski

● ●

49) What is the full name of the second Transformers movie?

50) WHAT IS THE FULL NAME OF THE THIRD TRANSFORMERS MOVIE?

51) Which *Mission: Impossible* film did J.J. Abrams, director of the *Star Trek* film, direct?

    a) Mission: Impossible
    b) Mission: Impossible II
    c) Mission: Impossible III
    d) All of the above

52) True or false: **Peter Sarsgaard, from *The Green Lantern* and *Knight and Day*, was born in Norway.**

* *

53) What was the name of James Franco's character in *Spider-Man?*
a) Harry Harold   b) Harry Robertson
c) Harry Harris   d) Harry Osborn

54) True or false: Three different actors played J.K. Simmons in the three Tobey McGuire *Spider-Man* films.

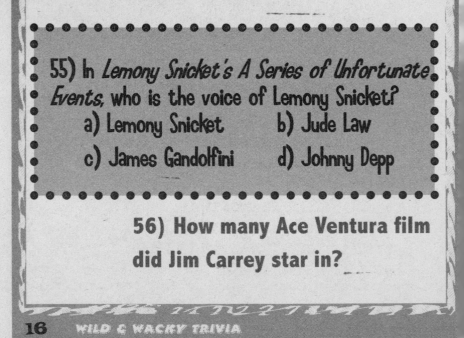

55) In *Lemony Snicket's A Series of Unfortunate Events,* who is the voice of Lemony Snicket?
a) Lemony Snicket   b) Jude Law
c) James Gandolfini   d) Johnny Depp

56) How many Ace Ventura film did Jim Carrey star in?

57) What Batman villain did Jim Carrey play in _Batman Forever?_

• •

58) Was the 1951 version of _A Christmas Carol_ starring Alastair Sim in color or black and white?

• •

59) Who was the voice of Mr. Fox in _The Fantastic Mr. Fox?_

* *

60) Who was the voice of Mrs. Fox in _The Fantastic Mr. Fox?_

• •

61) The mean farmers in _The Fantastic Mr. Fox_ are Boggis, Bunce, and _ _ _ _ _ _
a) Bligh   b) Bean   c) Bunch   d) Blech

62) BILL MURRAY STARRED IN A MODERN VERSION OF _A CHRISTMAS CAROL_ CALLED _ _ _ _ _ _ _ _ _?

A) _SCROOGED_   B) _MARLEY AND ME_

C) _TODAY'S CAROL_   D) _MERRY CHRISTMAS, MR. SCROOGE_

63) Complete the title of each of the following Mary-Kate and Ashley Olson movies.

   a) *It Takes* _____
   b) *Billboard* _____
   c) *Switching* _____
   d) *Passport to* _____
   e) *Our Lips are* _____

64) Which of the following movies did not feature a song performed by Justin Timberlake on its soundtrack?

   a) *Shark Tale*
   b) *Bad Boys II*
   c) *Love Actually*
   d) *The Sandlot*

65) True or false: The 2005 *King Kong* was the first time the 1930s classic film was remade?

****

66) True or false: Naomi Watts played Ann Darrow in *King Kong.*

67) True or false: There's a movie called: *Breakin'
3: Breakin It Old Skool.*

68) **True or false: There's a
movie called *Leonard, Part 6.***

69) **True or false:
Freaks and Geeks was a movie
before it was a TV show.**

70) Which was made first:
Teen Wolf or *Not Another Teen Movie?*

71) Which was made first:
*Confessions of a Teenage Drama
Queen* or *I Was a Teenage
Frankenstein.*

72) Have there been more *Land Before Time* movies or *Pink Panther* movies?

73) Have there been more *Rocky* movies or *Godzilla* movies?

● ● ● ● ● ● ● ● ● ● ● ● ● ● ● ● ● ● ● ●

74) HAVE THERE BEEN MORE *CHILD'S PLAY* MOVIES OR *NIGHTMARE ON ELM STREET* MOVIES?

● ● ● ● ● ● ● ● ● ● ● ● ● ● ● ● ● ● ● ●

75) The first company to advertise on TV sold...
- a) Food
- b) Clothes
- c) Watches
- d) Cars

76) Who does Jack McBrayer play on *30 Rock?*
- a) Kenneth Parcell
- b) Pete Hornberger
- c) Frank Rossitano
- d) Jack Donaghy

77) What is the name of the TV show-within-a-show on *30 Rock?*

    a) *FYI with Tracy Jordan*

    b) *PDQ with Tracy Jordan*

    c) *TGS with Tracy Jordan*

    d) *FAQ with Tracy Jordan*

78) What is "30 Rock" short for?

79) What show did Tina Fey leave to become a part of *30 Rock?*

80) Were there more episodes made of *Stargate SG1* or *Mission: Impossible?*

81) Were there more episodes made of *JAG* or *M*A*S*H?*

82) Were there more episodes made of *Friends* or *Married with Children?*

* *

83) How many seasons did The O.C. last?

84) What is the name of the adopted son in *The O.C.?*
    a) Robert
    b) Ryan
    c) Robin
    d) Richard

85) Which band did not appear on *The O.C.?*
    a) Death Cab for Cutie
    b) The Killers
    c) The Thrills
    d) Haircut 100

86) Which cable company has more subscribers, Comcast or Bright House Networks?

87) WHICH OF THE FOLLOWING IS NOT A NOW-DEFUNCT PREMIUM CHANNEL.

    A) SPOTLIGHT
    B) PRISM
    C) NIGHTLIGHT
    D) HOME THEATER NETWORK

• •

88) True or false: MSNBC used to be called America's Talking.

CHAPTER

2

Sports

89) Where did the Minnesota Twins play before moving to Minnesota?

90) WHERE DID THE LOS ANGELES DODGERS PLAY BEFORE MOVING TO LOS ANGELES?

91) Where did the Washington Nationals play before moving to Washington?

92) True or false: **The Atlanta Braves were once known as the Eagles.**

93) What outfielder twice finished third in the National League in stolen bases before retiring to become a prominent evangelist?

a) Billy Graham
b) Billy North
c) Billy Sunday
d) Billy Williams

94) In baseball, where did the Atlanta Braves play immediately before moving to Atlanta?

95) Match the team to its former stadium.
a) Briggs Stadium   1) Detroit Tigers
b) Candlestick Park   2) Minnesota Twins
c) Hubert H. Humphrey Metrodome 3) New York Mets
d) Shea Stadium   4) San Francisco Giants

96) How many no-hitters did Nolan Ryan pitch?

a) 4   b) 5   c) 6   d) 7

97) How many no-hitters did Roger Clemens pitch?
a) 0   b) 1   c) 2   d) 3

98) Who was the first Rookie of the Year?

99) What did Ted Williams do in his final at-bat?
a) Single   b) Double   c) Triple   d) Homer

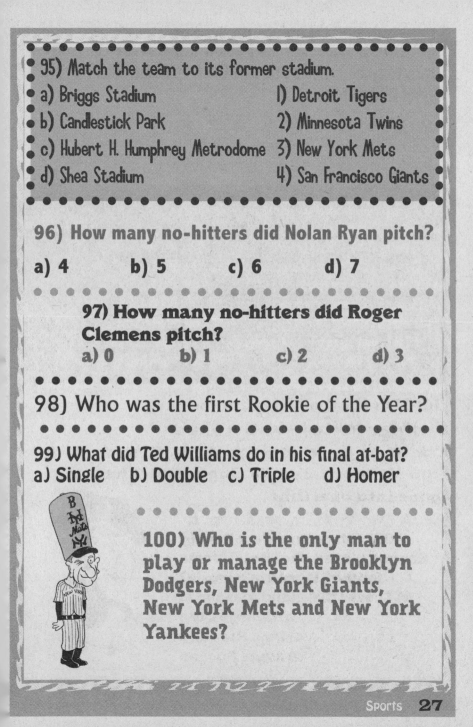

100) Who is the only man to play or manage the Brooklyn Dodgers, New York Giants, New York Mets and New York Yankees?

101) True or false: The 2011 Texas Rangers are the first team to come within one strike of winning the World Series and not win it.

★ ★ ★ ★ ★ ★ ★ ★ ★ ★ ★ ★ ★ ★ ★ ★ ★ ★

102) TRUE OR FALSE: THERE WAS NO WORLD SERIES IN 1994 BECAUSE OF A PLAYERS' STRIKE.

103) Match the owner to his team.

a) Gene Autry
b) George W. Bush
c) Charles Comiskey
d) Charlie Finley
e) George Steinbrenner
f) Ted Turner
g) Phil Wrigley
h) Tom Yawkey

1) Angels
2) A's
3) Braves
4) Cubs
5) Rangers
6) Red Sox
7) White Sox
8) Yankees

104) In football, who are the only brothers to both be drafted with the #1 pick?

★ ★ ★ ★ ★ ★ ★ ★ ★ ★ ★ ★ ★ ★ ★ ★ ★ ★

105) True or false: No Super Bowl has ever gone into overtime.

★ ★ ★ ★ ★ ★ ★ ★ ★ ★ ★

106) Future President Ronald Reagan played what Notre Dame football legend in a movie?
a) Grover Cleveland Alexander
b) George Gipp
c) Paul Hornung
d) Knute Rockne

107) Who was the NFL's first black player?
  a) Jim Brown
  b) Tony Dungy
  c) Fritz Pollard
  d) Jackie Robinson

108) Which city has never been home to an NFL franchise?
  a) Akron, OH
  b) Hammond, IN
  c) Racine, WI
  d) Wichita, KS

★ ★ ★ ★ ★ ★ ★ ★ ★ ★ ★ ★ ★ ★ ★ ★ ★

109) What Oakland Raiders owner was commissioner of the AFL?

★ ★ ★ ★ ★ ★ ★ ★ ★ ★ ★ ★ ★ ★ ★ ★ ★

110) What quarterback "guaranteed" a Super Bowl victory for the underdog New York Jets, and then delivered?

★ ★ ★ ★ ★ ★ ★ ★ ★ ★ ★ ★ ★ ★ ★ ★ ★

111) True or false: The Pittsburgh Steelers are the only team to win three straight Super Bowls.

112) What quarterback threw 420 touchdown passes, 2nd-most in NFL history, but never won a Super Bowl?
  a) Dan Marino
  b) Warren Moon
  c) Fran Tarkenton
  d) Johnny Unitas

113) Pro Bowl receiver Art Monk is a second cousin of what jazz legend?

114) MATCH THE NICKNAME TO THE PLAYER.

A) HOLLYWOOD   1. THOMAS HENDERSON

B) SNAKE   2. ED JONES

C) TOO MEAN   3. HARVEY MARTIN

D) TOO TALL   4. KEN STABLER

115) What was William Perry's nickname?

   a) The Refrigerator

   b) The Toaster

   c) The Burner

   d) The Microwave

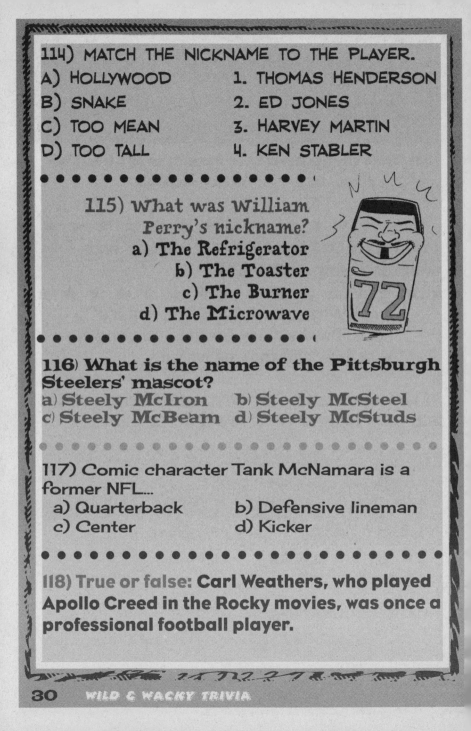

116) What is the name of the Pittsburgh Steelers' mascot?

a) Steely McIron   b) Steely McSteel

c) Steely McBeam   d) Steely McStuds

117) Comic character Tank McNamara is a former NFL...

   a) Quarterback   b) Defensive lineman

   c) Center   d) Kicker

118) True or false: **Carl Weathers, who played Apollo Creed in the Rocky movies, was once a professional football player.**

119) Match the NBA player to the country where he was born:

a) Pau Gasol   1) Nigeria
b) Yao Ming   2) Germany
c) Hakeem Olajuwon   3) Congo
d) Dirk Nowitzki   4) China
e) Dikembe Mutombo   5) Spain
f) Manu Ginobili   6) Argentina

120) Was the first professional basketball league created before or after 1900?

121) Which two teams did Kareem Abdul-Jabbar play for?

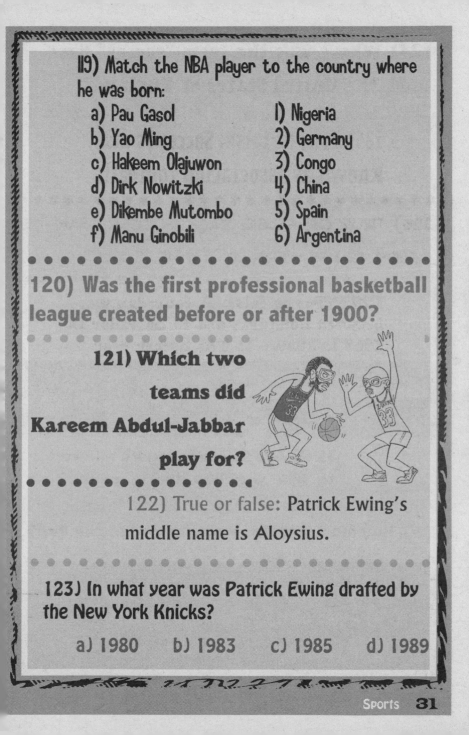

122) True or false: Patrick Ewing's middle name is Aloysius.

123) In what year was Patrick Ewing drafted by the New York Knicks?

a) 1980   b) 1983   c) 1985   d) 1989

124) Where was the term "soccer" first used, the United States or England?

* * * * * * * * * * * * * * *

125) True or false: Soccer is also known as association football.

* *

126) TRUE OR FALSE: EACH SOCCER TEAM FIELDS TEN PLAYERS AT A TIME.

* *

127) True or false: A four-day war between Honduras and El Salvador in 1969 is known as The Soccer War.

128) True or false: Iran once beat the U.S. in a World Cup match.

129) Are soccer players allowed to wear watches during games?

* * * * * * * * * * * * * * *

130) How many minutes in a standard soccer half?

131) A soccer player is "booked" if he or she has:
a) A red card   b) A yellow card
c) A blue card   d) A white card

132) True or false: Since 1984, professional soccer players have been allowed to compete in the Olympics.

133) True or false: Hockey pucks are frozen before put in play.

* *

134) True or false: A fighting penalty in hockey is four minutes.

* *

135) True or false: The first hockey puck was square.

* *

136) How many total players are on the ice for one team at one time (with no penalties)?

137) True or false: An NHL hockey puck is made of vulcanized rubber?

138) HOW MANY PLACES ON THE RINK CAN A FACE-OFF OCCUR?

139) Which usually has longer blades, a goaltender's skates or a forward's?

* *

140) In bowling, how many strikes in a row are considered a turkey?

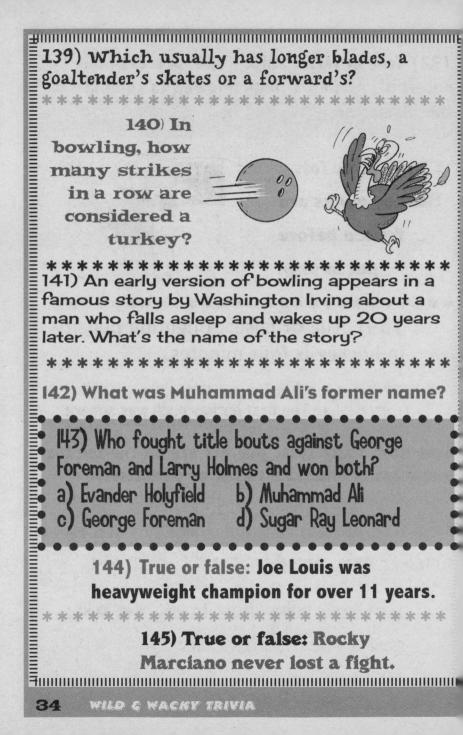

* *

141) An early version of bowling appears in a famous story by Washington Irving about a man who falls asleep and wakes up 20 years later. What's the name of the story?

* *

142) What was Muhammad Ali's former name?

143) Who fought title bouts against George Foreman and Larry Holmes and won both?
a) Evander Holyfield   b) Muhammad Ali
c) George Foreman   d) Sugar Ray Leonard

144) True or false: **Joe Louis was heavyweight champion for over 11 years.**

* *

145) True or false: Rocky Marciano never lost a fight.

146) Who came first, Sugar Ray Leonard or Sugar Ray Robinson?

147) Sugar Ray Robinson's success prompted what musician to change his name to avoid confusion, using his middle name professionally?

148) Is the band Sugar Ray named after Sugar Ray Leonard, Sugar Ray Robinson, or neither?

149) A fish is named after which heavyweight champ?

150) TRUE OR FALSE: RUGBY IS NAMED AFTER SIR. JOHN RUGBY OF DERBYSHIRE.

151) In rugby, how many points do you score for a try?

152) How many points do you score for a conversion kick?

● ●

153) How many points do you score for a penalty kick?

● ● ● ● ● ● ● ● ● ● ● ●

154) Which of the following is not a rugby position?
a) Flanker
b) Hooker
c) Eightman
d) Center

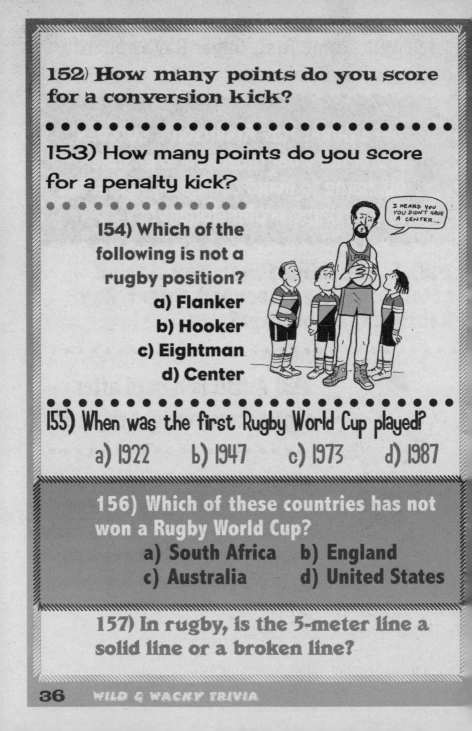

I HEARD YOU YOU DIDN'T HAVE A CENTER...

● ●

155) When was the first Rugby World Cup played?
a) 1922   b) 1947   c) 1973   d) 1987

156) Which of these countries has not won a Rugby World Cup?
a) South Africa   b) England
c) Australia   d) United States

157) In rugby, is the 5-meter line a solid line or a broken line?

158) Is the 22-meter line a solid line or a broken line?

159) Is the 10-meter line a solid line or a broken line?

160) How many players from each team gather in a scrum?

161) Should the ball hit the ground before it is kicked in a drop kick?

162) TRUE OR FALSE: NUMBERS ON RUGBY JERSEYS TELL YOU WHAT POSITION IS BEING PLAYED.

163) True or false: There are no kicking tees in rugby.

164) True or false: Archeologists have found ancient fishhooks used on the Nile.

165) True or false: The first sport-fishing handbook, *The Complete Angler*, was written in 1714.

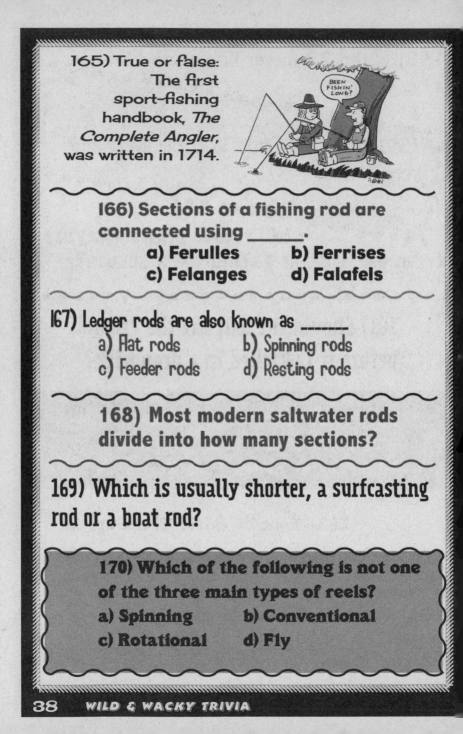

BEEN FISHIN' LONG?

166) Sections of a fishing rod are connected using _____.
a) Ferulles   b) Ferrises
c) Felanges   d) Falafels

167) Ledger rods are also known as _____
a) Flat rods   b) Spinning rods
c) Feeder rods   d) Resting rods

168) Most modern saltwater rods divide into how many sections?

169) Which is usually shorter, a surfcasting rod or a boat rod?

170) Which of the following is not one of the three main types of reels?
a) Spinning   b) Conventional
c) Rotational   d) Fly

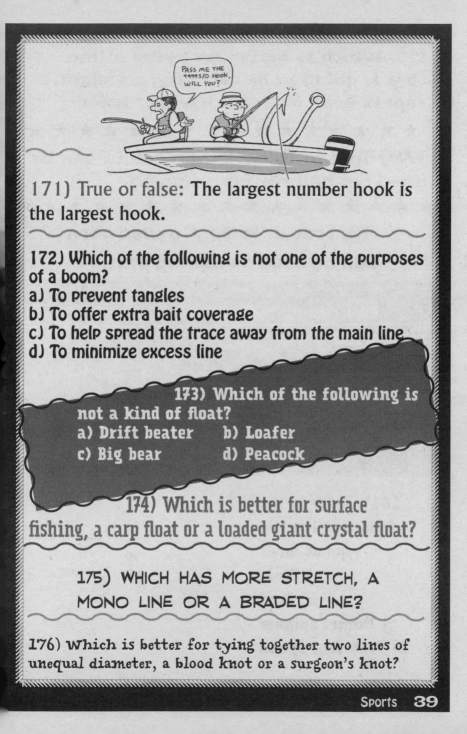

171) True or false: **The largest number hook is the largest hook.**

172) Which of the following is not one of the purposes of a boom?
a) To prevent tangles
b) To offer extra bait coverage
c) To help spread the trace away from the main line
d) To minimize excess line

173) Which of the following is not a kind of float?
a) Drift beater   b) Loafer
c) Big bear   d) Peacock

174) Which is better for surface fishing, a carp float or a loaded giant crystal float?

175) WHICH HAS MORE STRETCH, A MONO LINE OR A BRADED LINE?

176) Which is better for tying together two lines of unequal diameter, a blood knot or a surgeon's knot?

177) Which is better for tying a line that is going to be carrying a weight, a rapala knot or a shockleader knot?

★ ★ ★ ★ ★ ★ ★ ★ ★ ★ ★ ★ ★ ★ ★ ★ ★

178) True or false: Dog biscuits can be used for bait for carp fishing.

★ ★ ★ ★ ★ ★ ★ ★ ★ ★ ★ ★ ★ ★ ★ ★ ★

179) True or false: Canned corn can be used as fishing bait.

180) Peelers make good bait. These are crabs that...
- a) Are very young
- b) Are close to shedding their shells
- c) Are missing legs
- d) None of the above

181) Which of the following is not a type of lure?
- a) Ernie
- b) Burt
- c) Hornet spinner
- d) Professor spoon

182) Which of the following is not a type of lure?

   a) Zalt zam
   b) Taimenlippa spinner spoon
   c) Ace large flat flipper
   d) Deuce double flat spinner

183) Are vertical jigs used in surface or deepwater fishing?

184) Which of the following is not a type of fishing fly?

a) Adam's Parachute   b) Dads' Demoiselle
c) Hare's-ear Nymph   d) Captive Contessa

★ ★ ★ ★ ★ ★ ★ ★ ★ ★ ★ ★ ★ ★ ★ ★ ★

185) Who said, "Be patient and calm—for no one can catch a fish in anger"?

   a) Aristotle
   b) Herbert
      Hoover
   c) James
      Cameron
   d) Lady Gaga

PATIENCE!

Chow Time

186) True or false: The spiciest chili pepper in the world is the Trinidad Scorpion Butch T.

━━   ━━   ━━   ━━   ━━   ━━   ━━

187) True or false: There are more than 7,000 kinds of apples.

188) Which of the following is not a kind of apple?

    a) Fuji   b) Jonagold

    c) Green Delicious   d) Winesap

189) True of false: Apricot flowers are bright red.

━━   ━━   ━━   ━━   ━━   ━━   ━━

190) Do bananas grow on trees?

━━   ━━   ━━   ━━   ━━   ━━   ━━

191) True or false: Some cultures eat banana skins.

━━   ━━   ━━   ━━   ━━   ━━   ━━

192) Which has more calories, raisins or rhubarb?

193) Which has more calories, green beans or broccoli?

194) Which has more calories, cucumber or eggplant?

195) Which has more calories, horseradish or chives?

196) Which has more calories, lettuce or kale?

197) TRUE OR FALSE: AZTECS USED CHOCOLATE FOR RELIGIOUS AND MEDICAL REASONS, NOT FOR FOOD.

198) True or false:
The word "mole" as it is used in Mexican cooking, comes from the same source as the animal mole.

199) True or false: The Aztecs made guacamole.

200) True or false: The W.K. Kellogg Foundation was created in 1906 in an effort to help hospital patients digest food.

* * * * * * * * * * * * * * * * * *

201) In what state is Battle Creek, home of Kellogg's?

* *

202) What company produces Cheerios?

a) General Mills   b) Kellogg's

c) Kashi   d) None of the above

* *

203) True or false: Kix was the first puffed cereal.

* *

204) The forerunner of Taco Bell, Bell's Drive-In, primarily served what food?

205) Where is the Taco Bell Arena?

a) Boise, Idaho

b) Cleveland, Ohio

c) Springfield, Illinois

d) West Chester, Pennsylvania

206) True or false: Taco Bell serves French fries in Spain.

207) Hardee's is a sibling of what other restaurant chain?
a) Bob's Big Boy   b) Carl's Jr.
c) Jack in the box   d) Rally's

✳ ✳ ✳ ✳ ✳ ✳ ✳ ✳ ✳ ✳ ✳ ✳ ✳ ✳ ✳ ✳ ✳

208) McDonald's ads featured the Hamburglar. What rival chain used a similar character named Speedy McGreedy?

209) TRUE OR FALSE: TACO BELL GETS ITS NAME FROM THE MISSION-STYLE ARCHITECTURE FEATURING A BELL OVER THE FRONT DOOR.

210) What kind of dog starred in a series of commercials for Taco Bell?

✳ ✳ ✳ ✳ ✳ ✳ ✳ ✳ ✳ ✳ ✳ ✳ ✳ ✳ ✳ ✳ ✳ ✳ ✳ ✳

211) True or false: **Captain Kangaroo star Bob Keeshan was the first Ronald McDonald.**

✳ ✳ ✳ ✳ ✳ ✳ ✳ ✳ ✳ ✳ ✳ ✳ ✳ ✳

212) True or false: The name Arby's comes from the R in roast and the b in beef.

213) What does Burger King call its coffee?

214) Which has not been a Slurpee flavor:
- a) Super Sour Apple
- b) Bruisin Berry
- c) Dragon Fruit
- d) Cap'n Crunch

215) What game has been used in Subway promotions?
- a) Monopoly
- b) Scrabble
- c) Chutes and Ladders
- d) Boggle

216) True or false: There are more than 3,500 Applebee's restaurants.

217) What does TGI Friday's claim the TGI stands for?

218) What two color stripes are in the TGI Friday's logo?

219) Which is not a category of food at Noodles & Company?
a) Asian   b) African
c) Mediterranean   d) American

• •

220) Chili's line of hamburgers are called...
a) Double Dipping Burgers   b) Big Mouth Burgers
c) Power Burgers   d) Brother Burgers

• •

221) WHAT IS GIVEN FREE AT EVERY TEXAS ROADHOUSE TABLE?
A) OYSTER CRACKERS   B) CHEESE BALLS
C) PEANUTS   D) POPCORN

• •

222) True or false: Olive Garden was founded in Italy.

• •

223) True or false: General Mills launched Olive Garden.

• •

224) True or false: The décor in newer Oliver Garden restaurants is based on a specific house in Tuscany.

• •

225) The motto for Olive Garden is, "When you're here, you're _____."

226) True or false: Ruby Tuesday restaurants came before the Rolling Stones' song "Ruby Tuesday."

227) What are chicken fingers or strips at Long John Silver's called?

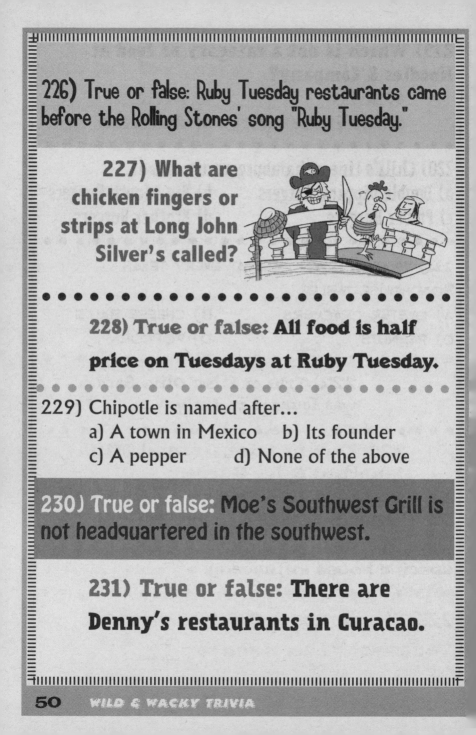

228) True or false: All food is half price on Tuesdays at Ruby Tuesday.

229) Chipotle is named after...
  a) A town in Mexico   b) Its founder
  c) A pepper   d) None of the above

230) True or false: Moe's Southwest Grill is not headquartered in the southwest.

231) True or false: There are Denny's restaurants in Curacao.

232) True or false: Denny's are open 24 hours.

233) TRUE OR FALSE: THE FIRST OF WHAT WOULD BE DENNY'S RESTAURANTS WAS CALLED DANNY'S DONUTS.

234) Was Denny's founded in the 1940s, the 1950s, or the 1960s?

235) True or false: **Every Chipotle restaurant is designed differently.**

236) True or false: Another name for ketchup used to be tomato soy.

237) In Denmark, mustard seed is used to ward off werewolves.

238) True or false: there is a National Mustard Museum.

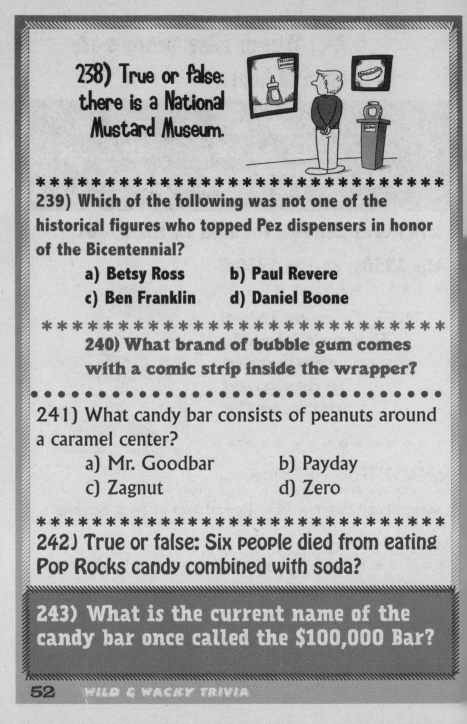

****

239) Which of the following was not one of the historical figures who topped Pez dispensers in honor of the Bicentennial?

    a) Betsy Ross   **b) Paul Revere**

    c) Ben Franklin   **d) Daniel Boone**

    ****

    240) What brand of bubble gum comes with a comic strip inside the wrapper?

• •

241) What candy bar consists of peanuts around a caramel center?

    a) Mr. Goodbar   b) Payday

    c) Zagnut   d) Zero

****

242) True or false: Six people died from eating Pop Rocks candy combined with soda?

243) What is the current name of the candy bar once called the $100,000 Bar?

244) What was the first Life Savers flavor?
 a) Pep-O-Mint   b) Spearmint
 c) Wild Cherry   d) Wint-O-Green

245) WHAT CHOCOLATE-COVERED NOUGAT BAR WAS NAMED AFTER A POPULAR DANCE?

* * * * * * * * * * * * * * *

246) True or false: Hershey's Kisses with both milk chocolate and white chocolate are called Hugs.

* * * * * * * * * * * * * * *

247) What candy bar features a bee on the wrapper?

248) The name of what candy bar is short for "twin sticks"?

249) True or false: Jelly Belly makes Dr. Pepper jelly beans.

CHAPTER

4

Game Time

250) True or false:
Each side of a Boggle cube contains only one letter.

251) True or false:
It's possible to form the word Inconsequentially in Boggle.

252) How many cube slots are there in a standard game of Boggle?

* *

253) How many cubes in Travel Boggle?

* *

254) What two numbers, between 1 and 12, are not featured on the cards in a game of Sorry!?

255) What is your other choice, besides moving ten spaces forward, when you draw a ten card in Sorry!

256) Of each player's 40 pieces in Stratego, how many are bombs?

* * * * * * * * * * * *

257) Of each player's 40 pieces in Stratego, how many are spies?

* *

258) How many blocks in a game of Jenga?

a) 48   **b) 54**   **c) 62**   **d) 72**

* *

259) How many of each color checkers are used in a game of backgammon?

* *

260) WHAT IS THE SECOND LOWEST NUMBER ON A BACKGAMMON DOUBLING CUBE?

* *

261) True or false: There is a Jewish edition of Apples to Apples.

* *

262) True or false: There is an **HBO** edition of Apples to Apples.

263) How many players can play Chinese Checkers at one time?

264) How many points do you get in Balderdash if you guess the correct definition?

265) How many points do you get in Balderdash if someone thinks your incorrect definition is correct?

266) How many diseases have broken out in the world in a basic game of Pandemic?

267) True or false: You can win a game of Wits and Wagers without knowing the answer to a single question.

268) Which of the following games is not played by Bill and Ted against Death in *Bill & Ted's Bogus Journey?*

a) Twister
b) Battleship
c) Candy Land
d) Electronic
   football

269) Is Dixit a card or dice game?

270) What level do you need to get to in order to win a basic game of Munchkin?

271) Which is not an edition of Scene It:
a) Glee edition   b) Seinfeld edition
c) Friends edition   d) Pretty Little Liars edition

272) THE GAME AXIS AND ALLIES IS SET DURING WHAT WAR?

273) How many players can play Guess Who? at one time?

274) Has there been a TV game show based on Taboo?

275) Which of the following objects is not a part of Mouse Trap?
a) A bathtub
b) A bucket
c) A boot
d) An anvil

276) What company originally published Dungeons and Dragons?

    a) Avalon Hill   b) Hasbro

    c) Milton Bradley   d) TSR

277) Absent magical enhancements, what is a character's maximum score for an ability?

278) Absent magical curses, what is the minimum score for an ability?

279) Can dead characters in D&D be revived?

280) Was there a Dungeons and Dragons movie?

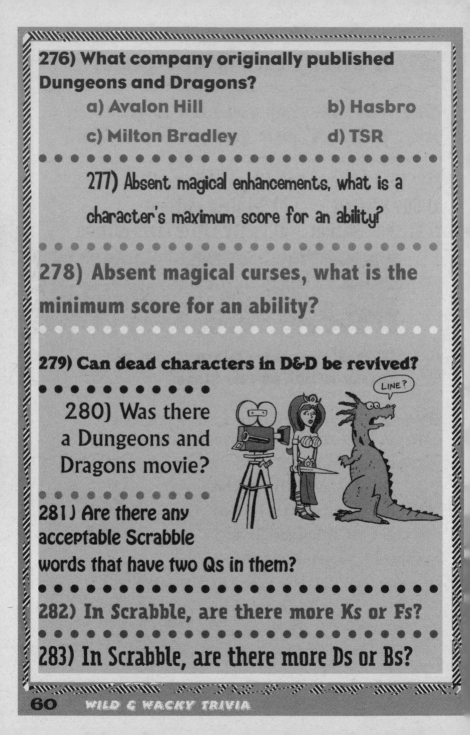

LINE?

281) Are there any acceptable Scrabble words that have two Qs in them?

282) In Scrabble, are there more Ks or Fs?

283) In Scrabble, are there more Ds or Bs?

284) WHICH OF THESE IS NOT ON RISK CARDS GIVEN AT THE END OF A SUCCESSFUL TURN?

    A) INFANTRY   B) CAVALRY

    C) AIRCRAFT   D) ARTILLERY

285) How many territory cards are there in Risk?

    a) 36   b) 42   c) 56   d) 62

286) If two players are playing Risk, how many armies does each player start with?

    a) 30   b) 40   c) 50   d) 60

287) Can you buy renter's insurance in the Game of Life?

288) Can you buy flood insurance?

289) Can you buy life insurance?

290) True or false: In the 1960's edition, you could end up at the Poor Farm.

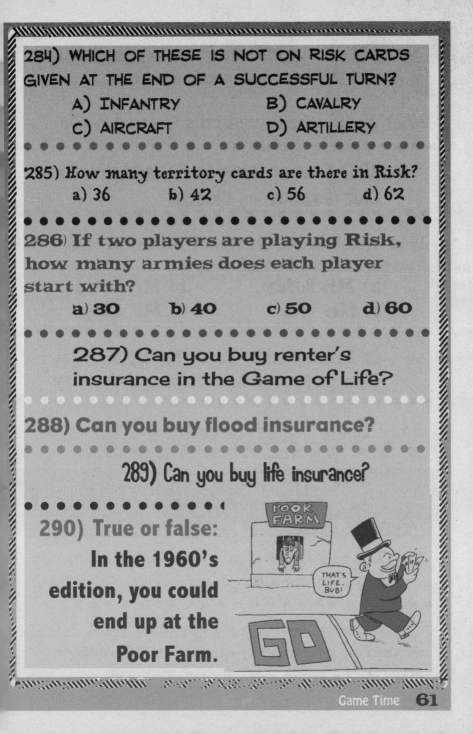

POOR FARM

THAT'S LIFE, BUB!

GO

291) True or false: The original Game of Life cars were convertibles.

292) What is the name of the Colonel in Clue?

293) True or false: In England, the game Clue is known as Cluedo.

294) What is the victim's name in the American version of Clue?

    a) Mr. Boddy   **b) Mr. Palid**

    c) Mr. Was   **d) Mr. Goner**

295) True or false: All of the properties in Monopoly are in Atlantic City, New Jersey.

296) DOES A MONOPOLY GAME CONTAIN MORE OR LESS THAN $12,000 IN PLAY MONEY?

297) True or false: Monopoly is available in more than 40 languages.

298) True or false: The longest recorded Monopoly game lasted more than 70 days.

299) True or false: A jeweler created a version of Monopoly valued at $12 million.

300) What game company was first to mass-market Monopoly?

    a) Hasbro   b) Ideal

    c) Milton Bradley   d) Parker Brothers

301) How many Monopoly properties can you reach by drawing a Chance card?

302) If you get out of jail by throwing doubles, do you get an extra turn?

303) Not counting the railroads and utilities, how many properties are named after neither states nor bodies of water?

304) True or false: an economics professor trying to illustrate the virtues of a free market over monopolies published a game called Anti-Monopoly.

305) True or false: Attorney Clarence Darrow invented Monopoly.

306) True or false: Rich Uncle Pennybags officially had his name changed to Mr. Monopoly by Parker Brothers.

307) In Zombie Tag (aka Gang Up or Minion Tag), what happens to the "It" person after he or she tags someone?

TAG. YOU'RE IT!

★ ★ ★ ★ ★ ★ ★ ★ ★ ★ ★ ★ ★ ★ ★ ★ ★ ★ ★

308) THE FOUR SQUARE WORLD CHAMPIONSHIP IS HELD IN...

    A) MAINE   B) MINNESOTA

    C) MARYLAND   D) MISSISSIPPI

★ ★ ★ ★ ★ ★ ★ ★ ★ ★ ★ ★ ★ ★ ★ ★ ★ ★

309) True or false: Students at Manchester College played Four Square for 120 hours to set a world record in 2011.

★ ★ ★ ★ ★ ★ ★ ★ ★ ★ ★ ★ ★ ★ ★ ★ ★

310) In competitive Four Square, are you allowed to spin the ball on a serve?

★ ★ ★ ★ ★ ★ ★ ★ ★ ★ ★ ★ ★ ★ ★ ★ ★ ★

311) In Four Square, is a ball that bounces on a line in or out?

★ ★ ★ ★ ★ ★ ★ ★ ★ ★ ★ ★ ★ ★ ★ ★ ★

312) What does the word bocce mean?

313) Is bocce an Olympic sport?

314) True or false: Kickball was originally called kick baseball?

315) Wiffle Ball was invented in the...
a) 1920s   b) 1930s   c) 1950s   d) 1970s

316) How many holes in a standard Wiffle Ball?

★ ★ ★ ★ ★ ★ ★ ★ ★ ★

317) What are the three basic pitches in Wiffle Ball?

318) In Wiffle Ball, what happens if a ball is caught in the air in fair territory?

319) How far is it from first to second base in an official Wiffle Ball game?
    a) 18 feet   b) 22 feet
    c) 28 feet   d) You don't need bases in an
                   official Wiffle Ball game

★ ★ ★ ★ ★ ★ ★ ★ ★ ★ ★ ★ ★ ★ ★ ★

320) HOW MANY WICKETS IN A STANDARD BACKYARD GAME OF CROQUET?

CHAPTER

5

Mother Earth

321) Meteorologist Alfred Wegener proposed in 1911 that the continents all were once one large land mass. What country was Wegener from?

322) Which of the following is not one of the major tectonic plates?
- a) Nazca Plate
- b) Pacific Plate
- c) Arctic Plate
- d) Indian Plate

323) What continent does the Nubia Plate largely include?

324) True or false: **Gravimetry measures gravitational force.**

325) **What is the name given to the supercontinent that existed in the late Paleozoic and early Mesozoic era?**
- a) Painglass
- b) Pangaea
- c) Penniless
- d) Prinus

326) True or false: Panthalassa is the name given to the global ocean that surrounded the land in the previous question.

327) **True or false:** Early seismographs used a pendulum to draw on glass or paper.

328) True or false: **Earthquakes under 2.0 on the Richter scale are perceivable by most people.**

329) How much more powerful is a 6.0 on the Richter scale than a 5.0?

    a) 1   b) 5   c) 10   d) 100

330) TRUE OR FALSE: THE 1995 EARTHQUAKE IN KOBE, JAPAN, IS THOUGHT TO BE THE ONE IN RECORDED HISTORY IN WHICH THE MOST PEOPLE DIED.

331) Modern skyscrapers should be able to withstand what level of earthquake as recorded on the Richter scale?

    a) 8.5   b) 8.7   c) 8.9   d) 9.3

332) True or false: **Seaquakes cause most tsunamis.**

333) True or false: There's a 37-mile-long magma chamber under New York City.

334) How long did it take for plants to start growing again after the eruption of Mount St. Helens?

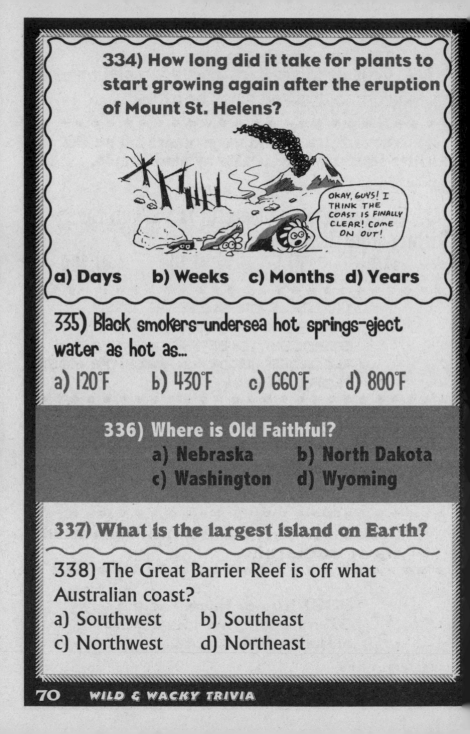

OKAY, GUYS! I THINK THE COAST IS FINALLY CLEAR! COME ON OUT!

a) Days   b) Weeks   c) Months   d) Years

335) Black smokers-undersea hot springs-eject water as hot as...

a) 120°F   b) 430°F   c) 660°F   d) 800°F

336) Where is Old Faithful?
    a) Nebraska   b) North Dakota
    c) Washington   d) Wyoming

337) What is the largest island on Earth?

338) The Great Barrier Reef is off what Australian coast?
a) Southwest   b) Southeast
c) Northwest   d) Northeast

339) About how many islands are in the Great Barrier Reef?

a) 100   b) 300   c) 600   d) 1,000

340) True or false: **The Yangtze is the longest river in Asia.**

341) When was the Saint Lawrence Seaway completed?

a) 1930s   b) 1940s   c) 1950s   d) 1960s

342) ABOUT WHAT PERCENTAGE OF THE EARTH'S SURFACE IS COVERED BY LAKES?

A) .5%   B) 1%   C) 2%   D) 4%

343) Where is the largest reservoir in the world?
a) United States   b) Ghana
c) China   d) Brazil

344) True or false: **Most salt lakes originally were filled with fresh water.**

345) Which is larger, a brook or a stream?

346) Which is larger, a creek or a stream?

347) Which is larger, a tributary or a branch?

★ ★ ★ ★ ★ ★ ★ ★ ★ ★ ★ ★ ★ ★ ★ ★ ★

348) Does a waterway begin or end at the head?

★ ★ ★ ★ ★ ★ ★ ★ ★ ★ ★ ★ ★ ★ ★ ★ ★

349) If a river is flowing west is the northern bank the right bank or the left bank?

350) What is the place where a fresh waterway empties into a salt-water body?

a) Estuary   b) Basin   c) Lock   d) Rift

351) Is Cairo on the banks of the Nile?

★ ★ ★ ★ ★ ★ ★ ★ ★ ★ ★ ★ ★ ★ ★ ★ ★

352) True or false: **More than half of the Nile is in Egypt.**

★ ★ ★ ★ ★ ★ ★ ★ ★ ★ ★ ★ ★ ★ ★ ★ ★

353) Is Egypt at the source or the mouth of the Nile?

354) THE NILE IS FORMED FROM THE WHITE NILE AND THE BLUE NILE. WHICH ONE COMES FROM ETHIOPIA?

355) Which is longer, the White Nile or the Blue Nile?

356) Is the Nile more likely to flood in August or February?

★ ★ ★ ★ ★ ★ ★ ★ ★ ★ ★ ★ ★ ★ ★ ★

357) Which of the following is not a dam on the Nile?

a) Sennar Dam   b) Aswan High Dam

c) Owen Falls Dam   d) East Cairo Dam

★ ★ ★ ★ ★ ★ ★ ★ ★ ★ ★ ★ ★ ★ ★ ★

358) True or false: There are places on the Mississippi River that are more than 180 feet deep.

★ ★ ★ ★ ★ ★ ★ ★ ★ ★ ★ ★ ★ ★ ★ ★

359) True or false: The name Mississippi comes from a Greek word.

★ ★ ★ ★ ★ ★ ★ ★ ★ ★ ★ ★ ★ ★ ★ ★

360) True or false: The Pontchartrain Causeway is the longest bridge over water in America.

★ ★ ★ ★ ★ ★ ★ ★ ★ ★ ★ ★ ★ ★ ★ ★

361) In what state is the source of the Mississippi?

362) Does the Mississippi River only flow in the U.S.?

363) Which of the following states doesn't have the Mississippi River running through it?
   a) Mississippi   b) Missouri
   c) Indiana d) Maryland

* *

364) Which is closer to the source of the Mississippi, Genoa Wisconsin or Hannibal, Missouri?

* *

365) Do any railroad tunnels go under the Mississippi River?

* *

366) TRUE OR FALSE: AMERIGO VESPUCCI WAS THE FIRST EUROPEAN TO REACH THE MISSISSIPPI RIVER.

367) True or false: The Mississippi River was once the border between the Spanish Empire and the British Empire.

368) True or false: The finless porpoise can be found in the Yangtze River.

369) True or false: The Yangtze River flows through four countries.

* *

370) In what country is the source of the Ob River?

* *

371) In what country is the source of the Yellow River?

* *

372) In what country is the source of the Yenisei River?

* *

373) True or false: Few fish live in the Great Salt Lake.

374) True or false: It is estimated that over 100 billion brine flies make their home at the Great Salt Lake.

375) Toledo, Ohio, is on what Great Lake?

* *

376) Which Great Lake is entirely within the United States?

377) The names of which two Great Lakes come from French words?

378) TRUE OR FALSE: MOUNT EVEREST IS CONSIDERED THE MOST DIFFICULT MOUNTAIN IN THE WORLD TO CLIMB.

379) True or false: More than 2,000 people have climbed Mount Everest.

380) True or false: **More than 1,000 people have died trying to climb Mount Everest.**

381) True or false: Mauna Kea in Hawaii is actually a bigger mountain than Mount Everest...if you measure it from its base, which is below sea level.

382) In 1978, Reinhold Messner and Peter Habeler were the first to make it to the top of Everest without supplemental _____.

383) In 2005, what did French pilot Didier Delsalle land on Everest?

384) True or false: **The oldest climber to reach the top of Everest was 92 years old.**

385) Which is higher: Dome Fuji Peak in Antarctica or K2 in Pakistan?

386) Which is higher: Kilimanjaro in Tanzania or Mt. McKinley in the U.S.

387) True or false: The Sassafras Mountains are in South Dakota.

388) What country named Mount Everest?
  a) The United States   b) China
  c) Nepal   d) England

389) True or false: **The people of Nepal called Mount Everest Chomolungma.**

390) OF THE TWO MAIN CLIMBING ROUTES UP MOUNT EVEREST, WHICH IS THE EASIEST TO CLIMB, THE SOUTHEAST RIDGE FROM NEPAL OR THE NORTHEAST RIDGE FROM TIBET?

391) What is the term for the line where an earthquake is more likely to hit?

392) The earthquake location where the earth first moved is called what?

393) The color-coded map that is used to determine how far-reaching an earthquake impacts is called what?

a) ShakeMap

b) QuakeMap

c) RichterMap

d) VibraMap

394) Which did more damage, the San Francisco earthquake of 1906 or the aftermath—which included looting and an ill-fated plan to dynamite buildings to create firebreaks.

395) In what state did the strongest U.S. earthquake occur?

      a) California   b) New Mexico

      c) Hawaii   d) Alaska

396) True or false: Of the top-10 earthquakes ever recorded, none took place in Europe or Africa.

CHAPTER

6

397) What is the mother cat's name in The *Aristocats?*
- a) Duchess
- b) Dainty
- c) Daliah
- d) Dorcett

398) WHICH OF THE FOLLOWING DISNEY PRINCESSES WAS NOT A PRINCESS BY BIRTH?
- A) SNOW WHITE
- B) BELLE
- C) JASMINE
- D) AURORA

399) Which Disney princess never technically became a princess by bloodline or marriage?
- a) Mulan
- b) Ariel
- c) Pocahontas
- d) Belle

400) Which princess has two living parents?
- a) Cinderella
- b) Ariel
- c) Snow White
- d) Mulan

401) True or false: One of the Disney princesses was voiced by a man.

402) Which of these Disney princesses wears a crown?
- a) Belle
- b) Cinderella
- c) Ariel
- d) Aurora

403) Which Disney princess has a tiger as a sidekick?

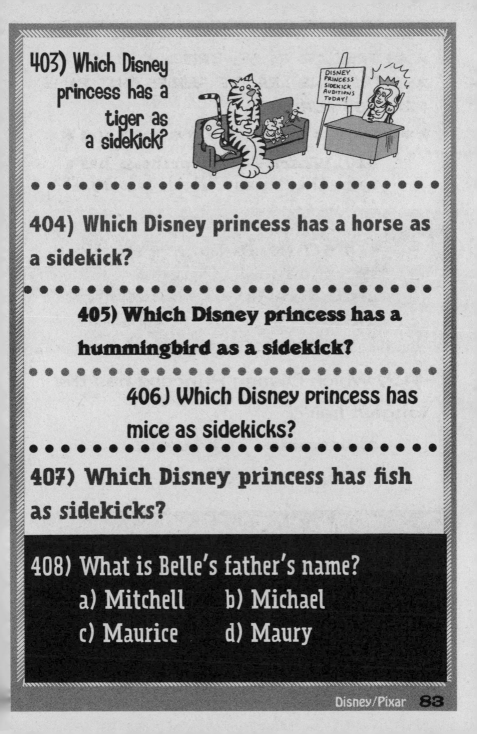

404) Which Disney princess has a horse as a sidekick?

405) Which Disney princess has a hummingbird as a sidekick?

406) Which Disney princess has mice as sidekicks?

407) Which Disney princess has fish as sidekicks?

408) What is Belle's father's name?
a) Mitchell   b) Michael
c) Maurice   d) Maury

409) TRUE OR FALSE: DRIZELLA, FLORA, AND TREMAINE ARE THE FAIRIES THAT RAISE PRINCESS AURORA.

* *

410) Which Disney princess has a name that means "little mischief"?

411) Which Disney princess has the most siblings?
a) Cinderella   b) Jasmine
c) Ariel   d) Mulan

412) Which Disney Princess has the longest hair?
a) Jasmine   b) Aurora
c) Rapunzel   d) Mulan

413) Which Disney princess sings "I want adventure..."?

414) Which Disney princess sings "Up where they stay all day in the sun"?

415) Which Disney princess sings "The dream that you wish will come true"?

416) Which Disney princess sings "the way you did once upon a dream"?

* *

417) Which Disney princess do we see as a baby?
      a) Cinderella   b) Snow White
      c) Aurora   d) Jasmine

418) Where does *Princess and the Frog* primarily take place?

419) True or false: *Tangled* is the first official Disney princess film without the proper name of a character in its title.

* * * * * * * * * * * * * * * * *

420) In *Tangled,* how long is Rapunzel's hair at maximum?
      a) 30 ft.   b) 50 ft.
      c) 70 ft.   d) 90 ft.

421) IN *TANGLED*, ARE THERE MORE ANIMATED THUGS OR TOWNSPEOPLE?

●●●●●●●●●●●●●●●●●●●●●●●●●

422) In *The Princess and the Frog*, where is Prince Naveen from?
    a) Caledonia   b) Maldonia
    c) Cardodia   d) Freedonia

●●●●●●●●●●●●●●●●●●●●●●●●●

423) In *The Princess and the Frog*, what is Tiana's debutante friend's name?
    a) Charlene   b) Charlotte
    c) Charmaine   d) Charla

●●●●●●●●●●●●●●●●●●●●●●●●●

424) Louis the Alligator in *The Princess and the Frog* is a tribute to what trumpet player:
    a) Louis Armstrong b) Louie Prima
    c) Louis Calhern   d) Louis L'Amour

425) What kind of business does Tiana open at the end of *The Princess and the Frog?*

426) What is the name of the firefly in *The Princess and the Frog?*

427) In *The Princess and the Frog,* what is Dr. Facilier also known as?
a) The Shadow Man
b) Lord of Darkness
c) Beast of the Moon
d) The Man from Beyond

428) True or false: In *The Princess and the Frog, Mama Odie can't speak.*

● ●

429) True or false: Oprah Winfrey supplied one of the voices in *The Princess and the Frog.*

● ● ● ● ● ● ● ● ● ● ● ●

430) What Disney film included the song "Give a Little Whistle"?

● ●

431) What Disney film included the song "Once Upon a Dream"?

● ● ● ● ● ● ● ● ● ● ● ● ● ● ● ● ● ● ● ●

432) What Disney film included the song "Bella Notte (This is the Night)"?

433) WHAT DISNEY FILM INCLUDED THE SONG "I'M LATE"?

434) What Disney film included the song "Baby Mine"?

435) What Disney film included the song "Everybody Wants to be a Cat"?

436) What Disney film included the song "Candle on the Water"?

437) What Disney film included the song "Friend Like Me"?

438) What Disney film included the song "Can You Feel the Love Tonight"?

439) What Disney film included the song "Go the Distance"?

440) What Disney film included the song "Reflection"?

441) What Disney film included the song "True Love's Kiss"?

442) What Disney film included the song "Hawaiian Roller Coaster Ride"?

443) What Disney film included the song "My Funny Friend and Me"?

444) What Disney film included the song "You'll Be in My Heart"?

445) WHAT DISNEY FILM INCLUDED THE SONG "COLORS OF THE WIND"?

446) What Disney film included the song "Part of Your World"?

447) What Disney film included the song "Be Our Guest"?

* * * * * * * * * * * * * * * * *

448) What Disney film included the song "Cruella De Vil"?

* * * * * * * * * * * * * * * * *

449) What Disney film included the song "The Second Star to the Right"?

450) What Disney film included the song "A Dream Is a Wish Your Heart Makes"?

451) What Disney film included the song "Little April Shower"?

* * * * * * * * * * * * * * * *

452) What Disney film included the song "God Help the Outcasts"?

453) What Disney film included the song "Trust in Me"?

★ ★ ★ ★ ★ ★ ★ ★ ★ ★ ★ ★ ★ ★ ★ ★ ★ ★

454) What Disney film included the song "I'm Wishing"?

★ ★ ★ ★ ★ ★ ★ ★ ★ ★ ★ ★ ★ ★ ★ ★ ★ ★

455) True or false: *Beauty and the Beast* and *The Little Mermaid* were released theatrically in the same year.

★ ★ ★ ★ ★ ★ ★ ★ ★ ★ ★ ★ ★ ★ ★ ★

456) Which of the following was not made at Disney Florida studio:
- a) *Lilo and Stitch*
- b) *Atlantic*
- c) *Mulan*
- d) *Brother Bear*

★ ★ ★ ★ ★ ★ ★ ★ ★ ★ ★ ★ ★ ★ ★ ★

457) TRUE OR FALSE: IN THE SHORT, *DER FUEHRER'S FACE*, DONALD DUCK LIVES IN NAZI GERMANY.

458) Was Donald Duck or Mickey Mouse part of the Three Caballeros?

459) What computer titan helped found Pixar?
a) Larry Ellison b) Bill Gates
c) Steve Jobs   d) Steve Wozniak

* * * * * * * * * * * * * * *

460) True or false: the villain in *A Bug's Life* is General Mandible.

* * * * * * * * * * * * * * *

461) What fuel is manufactured by Monsters, Inc.?

* * * * * * * * * * * * * * * * * * * *

462) What fuel do the monsters eventually discover is more energy-efficient?

* * * * * * * * * * * * *

463) True or false: The voice of the little girl in *Monsters, Inc.* was supplied by the 2-year-old daughter of one of the animators.

464) True or false: the only Oscars won by Pixar movies have been for Best Animated Feature.

* * * * * * * * * * * * * * * * * *

465) Did *Monsters, Inc.* win the Oscar for Best Animated Feature?

466) Did *Finding Nemo* win the Oscar for Best Animated Feature?

467) True or false: *Everybody Loves Raymond* co-stars Ray Romano and Brad Garrett both supplied the voices of fish in *Finding Nemo.*

* *

468) Did *The Incredibles* win the Oscar for Best Animated Feature?

* * * * * * * * * * * * * * * *

469) TRUE OR FALSE: HOLLY HUNTER WAS NOMINATED FOR BEST SUPPORTING ACTRESS FOR HER VOICE WORK IN *THE INCREDIBLES.*

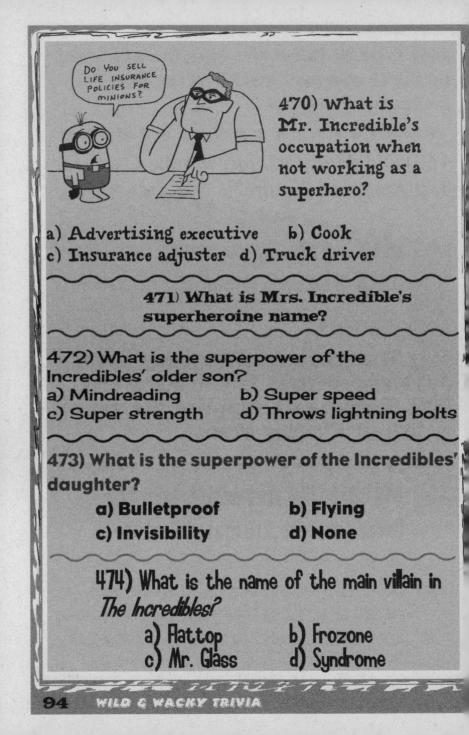

470) What is Mr. Incredible's occupation when not working as a superhero?

a) Advertising executive   b) Cook
c) Insurance adjuster d) Truck driver

471) What is Mrs. Incredible's superheroine name?

472) What is the superpower of the Incredibles' older son?
a) Mindreading   b) Super speed
c) Super strength   d) Throws lightning bolts

473) What is the superpower of the Incredibles' daughter?

a) Bulletproof   b) Flying
c) Invisibility   d) None

474) What is the name of the main villain in *The Incredibles?*
a) Flattop   b) Frozone
c) Mr. Glass   d) Syndrome

475) Did *Cars* win the Oscar for Best Animated Feature?

476) The plot of the classic Japanese movie *The Seven Samurai* is duplicated (somewhat) in what Pixar movie?

477) The plot of the Michael J. Fox movie *Doc Hollywood* is duplicated (somewhat) in what Pixar movie?

478) The plot of the 1991 action-comedy *If Looks Could Kill* is duplicated (somewhat) in what Pixar movie?

479) Did *Ratatouille* win the Oscar for Best Animated Feature?

480) Who supplies the voice of Colette, the chef who falls in love with the hero in Ratatouille?
a) Brigitte Bardot   b) Juliette Binoche
c) Catherine Deneuve   d) Janeane Garofalo

481) WHICH OF THESE WORDS RHYMES WITH "RATATOUILLE"?
A) FEEL   B) HOORAY
C) PHILLY   D) PHOOEY

482) Did *WALL-E* win the Oscar for Best Animated Feature?

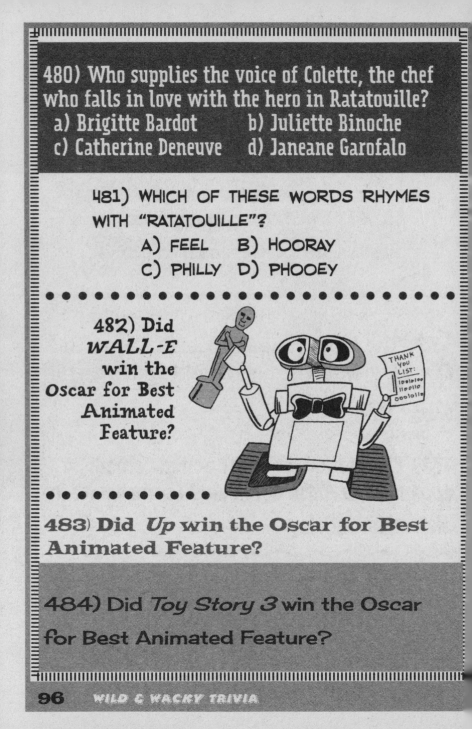

483) Did *Up* win the Oscar for Best Animated Feature?

484) Did *Toy Story 3* win the Oscar for Best Animated Feature?

485) What year was the first *Toy Story* released in movie theaters?
  a) 1990   b) 1993   c) 1995   d) 1998

486) True or false: Josh Whedon, creator of *Buffy the Vampire Slayer*, helped write the original *Toy Story*.

487) Who is seen first in *Toy Story*, Woody or Buzz?

488) What is the name of the pizza parlor/game room in *Toy Story*?

489) *Cars* was inspired in part by the landscapes along what famous highway?
  a) I-95   b) Pacific Coast Highway
  c) Route 66   d) U.S. 40

490) What is Sid's last name in *Toy Story*?
  a) Johnson   b) Philips
  c) Davis   d) Lasseter

491) In *Toy Story*, what kind of animal is Scud?

492) True or false: As originally written, *Toy Story*'s Woody was going to be a ventriloquist dummy.

★ ★ ★ ★ ★ ★ ★ ★ ★ ★ ★

493) TRUE OR FALSE: AS ORIGINALLY WRITTEN *TOY STORY*'S BUZZ LIGHTYEAR WAS GOING TO BE A CAVEMAN.

★ ★ ★ ★ ★ ★ ★ ★ ★ ★ ★ ★ ★ ★ ★ ★ ★ ★ ★

494) True or false: *Toy Story* was Tom Hanks' fourth animated film.

★ ★ ★ ★ ★ ★ ★ ★ ★ ★ ★ ★ ★ ★ ★ ★ ★

495) True or false: G.I. Joe appears in two scenes in *Toy Story*.

★ ★ ★ ★ ★ ★ ★ ★ ★ ★ ★ ★ ★ ★ ★ ★

496) What sitcom actor has supplied a voice in every Pixar movie?
a) David Foley   b) Brad Garrett
c) John Goodman   d) John Ratzenberger

★ ★ ★ ★ ★ ★ ★ ★ ★ ★ ★ ★ ★ ★ ★ ★

497) Who is the only actor to perform live (not animated) in a Pixar movie?
a) Tim Allen   b) Ed Asner
c) Tom Hanks   d) Fred Willard

498) What is the name of the desk lamp that forms the "I" in the Pixar logo?
a) Edison   b) Lumen   c) Luxo   d) Sherlock

★ ★ ★ ★ ★ ★ ★ ★ ★ ★ ★ ★ ★ ★ ★ ★ ★ ★

499) What is the primary ingredient in ratatouille?
a) Cabbage   b) Cheese   c) Eggplant   d) Rat

★ ★ ★ ★ ★ ★ ★ ★ ★ ★ ★ ★ ★ ★ ★ ★ ★ ★

500) True or false: in *Toy Story 2,* Buzz Lightyear is kidnapped by the Evil Emperor Zurg.

501) What is the name of Woody's horse in *Toy Story 2* and *Toy Story 3?*

502) True or false: Dinoco, the much-coveted sponsor in *Cars,* operates a gas station seen in *Toy Story.*

★ ★ ★ ★ ★ ★ ★ ★ ★ ★ ★ ★ ★ ★ ★ ★ ★ ★

503) What is WALL-E's favorite musical?
a) *Cats*   b) *Fiddler on the Roof*
c) *Hello, Dolly!*   d) *Singin' in the Rain*

504) In what small town does most of the action take place in *Cars?*

* * * * * * * * * * * * * * *

505) WHO WINS THE PISTON CUP IN *CARS?*

    A) FRANCESCO BERNOULLI

    B) CHICK HICKS

    C) LIGHTNING MCQUEEN

    D) STRIP "THE KING" WEATHERS

✳ ✳ ✳ ✳ ✳ ✳ ✳ ✳ ✳ ✳ ✳ ✳ ✳

506) Which real-life racecar driver does **NOT** voice a character in *Cars?*

a) Dale Earnhardt Jr.   b) Danica Patrick

c) Richard Petty   d) Michael Schumacher

* * * * * * * * * * * * * *

507) True or false: **the ladybug in *A Bug's Life* is male.**

* * * * * * * * *

508) Which city does NOT host a race in *Cars 2?*

    a) Berlin

    b) London

    c) Rome

    d) Tokyo

✳ ✳ ✳ ✳ ✳ ✳ ✳ ✳ ✳ ✳ ✳ ✳ ✳

509) **True or false:** former James Bond actor Timothy Dalton is the voice of superspy Finn McMissile in *Cars 2.*

510) Which model of car is NOT among the "lemons" trying to destroy the racecars in *Cars 2?*
a) Gremlin   b) Pacer   c) Pinto   d) Yugo

* *

511) A statue of what car is at the center of town in *Cars?*

a) Edsel   b) Model T
c) REO Speedwagon   d) Stanley Steamer

* * * * * * * * * * * * * * * *

512) How many times did Doc Hudson win the Piston Cup?

a) 0   b) 1   c) 2   d) 3

* * * * * * * * * * * * * * * *

513) What notorious destroyer of toys lives next door to Andy in *Toy Story?*

a) Bonnie   b) Charlie   c) Johnny   d) Sid

* * * * * * * * * * * * * *

514) By the time of *Toy Story 3,* Andy's neighbor has a job as what?
a) Busboy   b) Garbage man
c) Gas-station attendant   d) Paperboy

* * * * * * * * * * * * * * *

515) What is Lightning McQueen's catchphrase?
a) Bazinga!   b) Ka-chigga ka-chigga!
c) Ka-chow!   d) Zoom zoom!

516) In the Pixar short _Presto,_ a magician's rabbit refuses to come out of the hat unless he gets what?

a) A carrot
b) A girlfriend
c) A raise
d) A vacation

517) ACTOR AND COMEDIAN DAN WHITNEY, A NOTABLE VOICE IN TWO PIXAR FEATURES AND SEVERAL SHORTS, IS BETTER KNOWN BY WHAT NAME?

****

518) Pixar made a series of shorts for the Disney Channel featuring Lightning McQueen and Mater under what umbrella title?

519) What veteran songwriter and pianist had been nominated for 14 Oscars and lost them all before winning for the song "If I Didn't Have You" from *Monsters, Inc.?*
a) Elton John
b) Diana Krall
c) Alan Menken
d) Randy Newman

520) True or false: Pixar founder John Lasseter was a Jungle Cruise captain at Disneyland.

521) What was the name of John Lasseter's attention-getting early short film?
a) *Luxo*
b) *Luxo Jr.*
c) *Luxo Sr.*
d) *Mister Luxo*

CHAPTER

7

Celebrities

522) John Mellencamp's first four albums were recorded under what name?

523) What is singer Fergie's full name?

524) What is writer William Sydney Porter better known as?

    a) O. Henry   b) Mark Twain

    c) Stephen King   d) R. L. Stein

525) Samuel Clemens is better known as whom?

526) Reginald Dwight is better known as what singer?

527) Match the initials to the name.

a) A.A.	1) NBA star Green
b) A.C.	2) Confederate general Hill
c) A.E.	3) Poet Housman
d) A.J.	4) Actress Michalka
e) A.M.	5) Author Milne
f) A.P.	6) Journalist Rosenthal

528) True or false: Comedian W.C . Fields' given names were Warren Corbett.

529) TRUE OR FALSE: C.C. SABATHIA'S GIVEN NAMES ARE CARSTEN CHARLES.

530) True or false: O.J. Simpson's given names are Oliver Jameson.

531) True or false: The C in J.C. Penney stands for Cash.

532) True or false: James Hoffa, whose disappearance in 1975 remains a mystery to this day, had the middle name Riddle.

533) What basketball player changed his name to Metta World Peace?

534) Dino Crocetti and Joseph Levitch are better known as what comedy team?

a) Martin and Lewis

b) Laurel and Hardy

c) Burns and Allen

d) None of the above

* * * * * * *

535) True or false:

Benny Kubelsky is better known as comedian Jack Benny.

* * * * * * * * * * * * * *

GOODNIGHT, GRACIE!

536) True or false:

Nathan Birnbaum is better known as comedian George Burns.

* * * * * * * * * * * * *

537) True or false: Ellas Otha Bates is better known as The Big Bopper.

538) Charles Addams: Cartoonist or signer or the Declaration of Independence?

* * * * * * * * * * *

539) Jim Morrison: Rock musician or Harry Truman's vice president?

540) Arthur Schopenhauer: Physician or philosopher?

541) JOHN WESLEY: METHODIST MINISTER OR FOUNDER OF HARVARD?

* * * * * * * * * * * * * * * *

542) John Maynard Keynes: Economist or ecologist?

543) Alfred North Whitehead: Beatles manager or mathematician?

544) William Wallace: The "Guardian of Scotland" or director of *The Wizard of Oz?*

545) Emiliano Zapata: Mexican revolutionary leader or J-Lo's first husband?

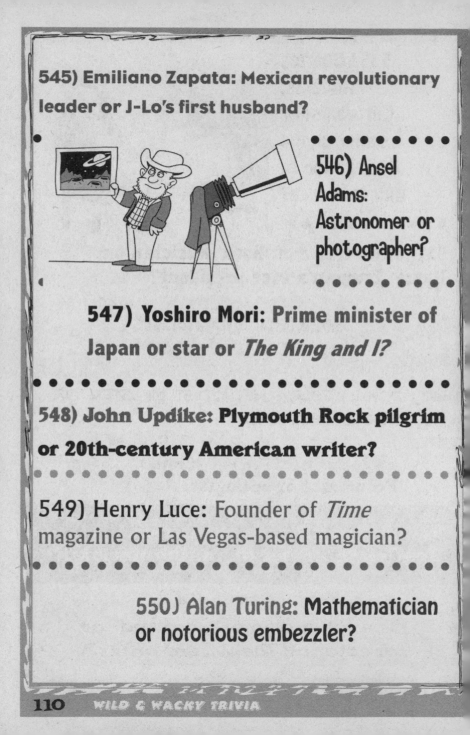

546) Ansel Adams: Astronomer or photographer?

547) Yoshiro Mori: Prime minister of Japan or star or *The King and I?*

548) John Updike: Plymouth Rock pilgrim or 20th-century American writer?

549) Henry Luce: Founder of *Time* magazine or Las Vegas-based magician?

550) Alan Turing: Mathematician or notorious embezzler?

551) Jack Welch: Chairman of GE or creator of the War of the Worlds hoax?

552) Billy Mays: Commercial pitchman or baseball star?

553) ARE SINGERS JOHN AND JULIAN LENNON RELATED?

554) Are ventriloquist Edgar Bergen and actress Candice Bergen related?

555) Are talk-show host Conan O'Brien and newswoman Soledad O'Brien related?

556) Are Confederate general Jeb Stuart and Watergate conspirator Jeb Stuart Magruder related?

557) True or false: *Lord of the Rings* actor Sean Astin is the son of *Addams Family* actor John Astin.

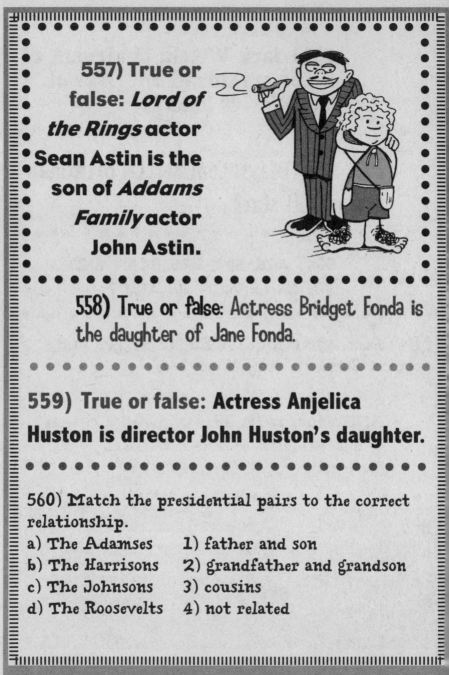

558) True or false: Actress Bridget Fonda is the daughter of Jane Fonda.

559) True or false: Actress Anjelica Huston is director John Huston's daughter.

560) Match the presidential pairs to the correct relationship.

a) The Adamses   1) father and son
b) The Harrisons   2) grandfather and grandson
c) The Johnsons   3) cousins
d) The Roosevelts   4) not related

561) Are talk-show host Morton Downey Jr. and actor Robert Downey Jr. related?

562) Are inventors Wilbur and Orville Wright related to architect Frank Lloyd Wright?

563) Natalia Zakharenko is better known as whom?

564) True or false: Writer P.G. Wodehouse's given names were Pelham Grenville.

565) Match the initials to the name.
a) D.A.   1) Hijacker Cooper
b) D.B.   2) Running back Dozier
c) D.H.   3) Comedian Hughley
d) D.J.   4) Author Lawrence
e) D.L.   5) Filmmaker Pennebaker

CHAPTER

8

★★★★★★★★★★

Music

566) Who sang "Brown Sugar" (1988)?

• • • • • • • • • • • • • • • • • • • •

567) WHO SANG "IMAGINE" (1971)?

• • • • • • • • • • • • • • • • • • • •

568) Who sang "Superstition" (1972)?

• • • • • • • • • • • • • • • • • • • •

569) Who sang "Losing My Religion" (1991)?

570) Who sang "Brown Eyed Girl" (1967)?

571) Who sang "Oh, Pretty Woman" (1964)?

a) The Rolling Stones　　**b) The Who**

c) Roy Orbison　　**d) Roy Acuff**

572) Who sang "What's Goin' On" (1971)?
a) Marvin Gaye　　b) Michael Bolton
c) Mahalia Jackson　　d) Michael Jackson

573) Who sang "Go Your Own Way" (1976)?

574) Who sang "When Doves Cry" (1984)?

575) Who sang "Bohemian Rhapsody" (1975)?

576) Who sang "(Sittin' On) The Dock of the Bay" (1968)?
- a) Otis Day and the Knights
- b) An Elevator Called Otis
- c) Otis Redding
- d) Helen Reddy

577) Who sang "Born to Run" (1975)?

578) Who sang "Waterfalls" (1995)?

579) WHO SANG "IRIS" (1998)?

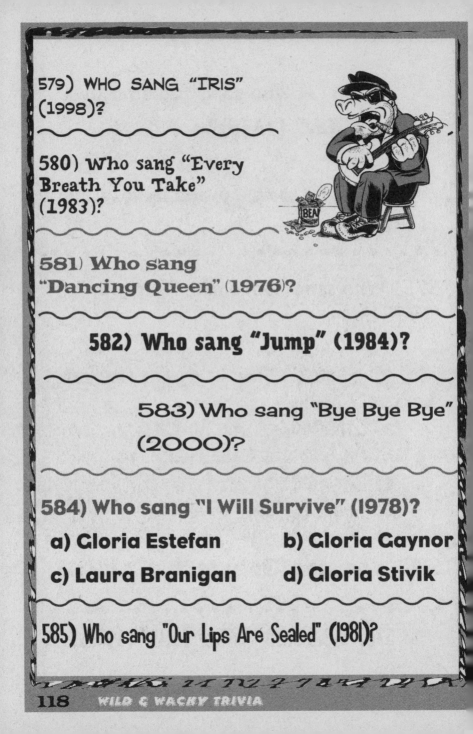

580) Who sang "Every Breath You Take" (1983)?

581) Who sang "Dancing Queen" (1976)?

582) Who sang "Jump" (1984)?

583) Who sang "Bye Bye Bye" (2000)?

584) Who sang "I Will Survive" (1978)?

a) Gloria Estefan   b) Gloria Gaynor

c) Laura Branigan   d) Gloria Stivik

585) Who sang "Our Lips Are Sealed" (1981)?

586) Who sang "Just the Way You Are" (1978)?

587) Who sang "Papa Don't Preach" (1986)?

588) Who sang "Benny and the Jets" (1973)?

589) Who sang "Time After Time" (1984)?

590) Who sang "My Name Is" (1999)?

591) True or false: Buddy Holly was 22 when he died in a plane crash.

592) WAS *CRY OF LOVE* RELEASED BEFORE OR AFTER JIMI HENDRIX' DEATH?

593) True or false: More than 2 million Michael Jackson albums have sold since his death.

594) Are the words "Bohemian" or "Rhapsody" in Queen's song "Bohemian Rhapsody?

****
595) Is the phrase "Sympathy for the Devil" in the Rolling Stones song "Sympathy for the Devil"?

****
596) Is the word "Australia" in the Shins' song "Australia"?

597) What is the parenthetical addition to the title for the Green Day song "Good Riddance"?

598) What is the parenthetical addition to the title for the Bryan Adams song "I Do It For You"?

599) What is the parenthetical addition to the title for the Simple Minds song "Don't You"?

600) Where are people supposed to face if "The Star Spangled Banner" is playing and there is no flag visible?

601) Who messed up the lyrics to "The Star Spangled Banner" before Super Bowl XLV?

a) Christina Aguilera b) Britney Spears

c) Fergie   d) Mama Cass

* *

602) Which of the following parts of "The Star Spangled Banner" lyrics were used as the name of a movie:
a) *Twilight's Last Gleaming*
b) *Home of the Brave*
c) *So Proudly We Hail*
d) *Stripes and Bright Stars*

603) True or false: "God Bless America" originally included the lyric "...to the right with a light from above."

604) TRUE OR FALSE: THE FIRST LINES OF "GOD BLESS AMERICA" ARE "GOD BLESS AMERICA/LAND THAT I LOVE."

605) What hockey team, throughout the 1970s, played Kate Smith's version of "God Bless America" for the Broad Street Bullies and their fans?

606) Who usually sings "God Bless America" at the beginning of the Indianapolis 500?
a) Florence Henderson (the *Brady Bunch* mom)
b) Shirley Jones (the *Partridge Family* mom)
c) Marion Ross (the *Happy Days* mom)
d) Esther Rolle (the *Good Times* mom)

607) Daniel Rodriguez' post-9/11 version of "God Bless America" made it onto the Billboard Hot 100. What was Rodriguez's regular job?

    a) Firefighter
    b) Police officer
    c) Ambulance driver
    d) Construction worker

• •

608) Who benefits from royalties for the song "God Bless America"?

    a) Girl Scouts and Boy Scouts
    b) Keep America Beautiful
    c) The American Red Cross
    d) The estate of Irving Berlin

• •

609) True or false: The same person who wrote "You're a Grand Old Flag" wrote "Yankee Doodle Dandy."

• •

610) True or false: Sales of "You're a Grand Old Flag" sheet music topped one million copies.

611) True or false: "You're a Grand Old Flag" was originally called "You're a Grand Old Rag."

612) True or false: "You're a Grand Old Flag" has the first reference ever to Uncle Sam.

★ ★ ★ ★ ★ ★ ★ ★ ★ ★ ★ ★ ★ ★ ★ ★ ★ ★ ★

613) True or false: Katharine Lee Bates wrote the music and lyrics for "America the Beautiful."

★ ★ ★ ★ ★ ★ ★ ★ ★ ★ ★ ★ ★ ★ ★ ★ ★ ★ ★

614) True or false: The lyrics to "America the Beautiful" were originally written as a poem called "Pikes Peak."

★ ★ ★ ★ ★ ★ ★ ★ ★ ★ ★ ★ ★ ★ ★ ★ ★ ★

615) Where was Katharine Lee Bates a professor when she wrote the lyrics for "America the Beautiful"?

a) Princeton   b) Harvard

c) Wellesley   d) University of Delaware

616) TRUE OR FALSE: "AMERICA THE BEAUTIFUL" DID NOT BECOME POPULAR UNTIL AFTER KATHARINE LEE BATES HAD DIED.

617) Which of the following did not appear on the all-star country version of "America the Beautiful" that was recorded in 2001.
a) Toby Keith
b) Keith Urban
c) Billy Ray Cyrus
d) Trace Adkins

★ ★ ★ ★ ★ ★ ★ ★ ★ ★ ★ ★ ★ ★ ★

618) Was the country-star version of "America the Beautiful" from the above question recorded before or after the 9/11 attacks?

★ ★ ★ ★ ★ ★ ★ ★ ★ ★ ★ ★ ★ ★ ★

619) Who performed a duet with Ray Charles on "America the Beautiful" on his *Genius & Friends* album?
a) Martina McBride
b) Alicia Keys
c) Amy Winehouse
d) Cobie Caillat

620) What movie star narrated the 1970 animated holiday special "Santa Claus is Comin' to Town"?

a) Gene Kelly   b) Donald O'Connor

c) Fred Astaire   d) Ginger Rogers

* *

621) In its original Broadway musical plot context, what is "Yankee Doodle"?

a) A solider   b) A horse   c) A statue   d A sports team

* *

622) True or false: The name of a Tom Cruise movie comes from the song "Yankee Doodle Dandy."

* *

623) True or false: Paul Jabara recorded a disco version of "Yankee Doodle Dandy."

624) Who starred in the movie "Yankee Doodle Dandy"?

a) Humphrey Bogart b) James Cagney
c) Edward G. Robinson d) James Stewart

• •

625) What Christmas carol is mentioned in Charles Dickens's *A Christmas Carol?*

    a) "God Rest Ye Merry, Gentlemen"
    b) "Jingle Bells"
    c) "Frosty the Snowman"
    d) "The Christmas Song"

626) In "Good King Wenceslas," reference is made to the Feast of Stephen. What day is that?

    a) The day after Christmas
    b) The day before Christmas
    c) The twelfth day of Christmas
    d) December 1st

627) On what record label did Kanye West originally produce music for Jay-Z and Alicia Keys?

    a) Roc-A-Billy Records
    b) Roc-A-Fella Records
    c) Roc-Da-House Records
    d) Roc-N-Out Records

628) When was Kanye West's first album released?
 a) 1996   b) 2000 c) 2004 d) 2006

629) Which Kanye West album came first, *Graduation* or *The College Dropout?*

630) WHAT RECORD LABEL, RUN BY KANYE WEST, ALSO RECORDED JOHN LEGEND?
 A) GREAT MUSIC   B) GOOD MUSIC
 C) OKAY MUSIC   D) COOL MUSIC

631) Where was Kanye West born?
 a) Atlanta   b) Philadelphia
 c) Washington, D.C.   d) Boston

632) True or false: Kanye West was featured on the "Glow in the Dark" tour.

633) Who is older, Coolio or Snoop Dogg?

634) True or false: "Gangsta's Paradise" was written for the movie "Dangerous Minds."

635) "Gangsta's Paradise" samples the song "PastLanyardime Paradise" by what artist?
a) Michael Jackson   b) Stevie Wonder
c) Ike Turner   d) Marvin Gaye

636) True or false: MC Hammer's "U Can't Touch This" samples Rick James' "Super Freak."

637) True or false: Ke$ha's "Right Round" samples Dead or Alive's "You Spin Me Round (Like a Record)."

638) True or false: Kid Rock's "All Summer Long" samples "Warren Zevon's "An American Werewolf in London."

639) True or false: Kid Rock's "All Summer Long" samples Lynyrd Skynyrd's "Sweet Home Alabama."

640) What group was Lisa "Left-Eye" Lopes a part of?
 a) TLC   b) Run-DMC
 c) KRS-One   d) G-Unit

641) True or false: Katy Perry's real name is Katheryn Elizabeth Hudson.

642) TRUE OR FALSE: KATY PERRY APPEARED IN THE MOVIE *THE SISTERHOOD OF THE TRAVELING PANTS.*

643) Who is featured with Katy Perry on the song "ET"?

644) How old was Avril Lavigne when her album Let Go released?

645) True or false: Avril Lavigne wrote theme songs for Tim Burton's *Alice in Wonderland*, *Charlie and the Chocolate Factory*, and *Planet of the Apes.*

646) True or false: Lil Wayne and Busta Rhymes are both featured on Chris Brown's "Look at Me Now."

647) True or false: Bruno Mars was raised in Hawaii.

648) True or false: In 1992, Bruno Mars appeared as a character named Little Elvis in the movie *Honeymoon in Vegas.*

649) What country singer's name was the title of Taylor Swift's first hit single?

650) True or false: Taylor Swift is the youngest person to be named Entertainer of the Year at the Country Music Association Awards.

651) What musician is the subject of each of these biographical films.

a) *Coal Miner's Daughter*   1) Jerry Lee Lewis

b) *La Bamba*   2) Richie Valens

c) *Walk the Line*   3) Loretta Lynn

d) *Great Balls of Fire*   4) Tina Turner

e) *What's Love Got to Do With It*   5) Johnny Cash

652) What musician is the subject of each of these biographical films.

a) *Ray*
b) *Sid and Nancy*
c) *Why Do Fools Fall in Love*
d) *Sweet Dreams*
e) *Nowhere Boy*

1) Sid Vicious
2) Frankie Lymon
3) John Lennon
4) Ray Charles
5) Patsy Cline

653) Who sang "Respect" (1967)?

* *

654) WHO SANG "WITH OR WITHOUT YOU" (1987)?

* *

655) Who sang "Hotel California" (1976)?

* * * * * * * * * * * * * * *

656) Who sang "I Want It That Way" (1999)?

* *

657) Who sang "Where Did Our Love Go" (1964)?

658) What band parodied the Beatles in two full-length mockumentaries, *All You Need Is Cash* and *Can't Buy Me Lunch?*

659) Fake folk-music groups The Folksmen, Mitch and Mickey, and the New Main Street Singers are the subject of what mockumentary?

660) David St. Hubbins, Derek Smalls, and Nigel Tufnel comprise what band?

* *

661) How many Top 40 singles did the Beatles have after John Lennon's death?

a) 1

b) 2

c) 3

d) 4

662) How many solo Top 40 singles did John Lennon have after his death?

   a) 1   b) 2   c) 3   d) 4

663) True or false: "**God Bless America**" was originally written to be part of a musical comedy revue.

664) True or false: "This Land in Your Land" was originally called "God Blessed America for Me."

665) In "This Land is Your Land," the singer saw the endless skyway above. What was seen below?

666) TRUE OR FALSE: BRUCE SPRINGSTEEN RECORDED A VERSION OF "THIS LAND IS YOUR LAND."

667) True or false: The lyrics for "The Star Spangled Banner" were written by an 18-year old.

• •

668) True of false: The lyrics for "The Star Spangled Banner" come from a poem called "Defense of Fort McHenry."

• •

669) What body of water does Fort McHenry overlook?

a) Delaware River   b) Chesapeake Bay

c) Atlantic Ocean   d) Gulf of Mexico

• •

670) When did "The Star Spangled Banner" become the U.S. National anthem?

a) 1822   b) 1931   c) 1965   d) 1979

671) True or false: "My Country, 'Tis of Thee" has the same melody as the British national anthem "God Save the Queen."

● ●

672) True or false: Lynyrd Skynyrd, Barry Manilow, and Dolly Parton all recorded versions of "Rudolph the Red-nosed Reindeer"

● ●

673) Which of the following opera titles are named for a character in it?

a) *Aida*

b) *La Boheme*

c) *Falstaff*

d) *La Traviata*

e) *Turendot*

674) True or false: The first million-selling record was of an opera aria.

• •

675) "Fidelio" is the only opera by Bach, Beethoven, or Brahms?

• •

676) What composer is the subject of the play and movie Amadeus?

• •

677) Who wrote the opera *Carmen?*
a) Bizet   b) Beethoven   c) Brahms   d) Bach

• •

678) CAMILLE SAINT-SAENS WROTE "CARNIVAL OF THE _____"?

• •

679) Who wrote the music for "Peer Gynt"?
a) Grieg   b) Gregg   c) Grogg   d) Grugg

• •

680) What Disney movie featured Moussorgsky's "Night on Bald Mountain"?

681) A lot of orchestras play this Tchaikovsky work on the 4th of July, but it's not inspired by the American Revolution but by a different war. What's the work called?

* * * * * * * * * * * * * *

682) Rossini's "William Tell Overture" is well known as the theme song for what cowboy hero?

* * * * * * * * * * * * * *

683) How many parts make up Wagner's Ring Cycle?

* *

684) Which of the following was not one of opera's famed "Three Tenors"?

a) Jose Carreras b) Luciano Pavarotti

c) Placido Domingo d) Enrico Caruso

685) What conductor of the New York Philharmonic also wrote the music for the Broadway musical *West Side Story?*

a) Leonard Bernstein b) Richard Rodgers

c) Stephen Sondheim d) Riccardo Muti

****

686) A requiem is a piece of music written for what?

****

687) What legendary Philadelphia symphony conductor led the orchestra in Disney's *Fantasia?*

a) Leopold Stokowski b) Leonard Bernstein

c) Larry David d) Lenny Bruce

****

688) What was legendary soprano Beverly Sills' nickname?

a) Bongles b) Bubbles
c) Baubles d) Babbles

****

689) True or false: **Ludacris's "Coming 2 America" samples Mozart's "Requiem."**

690) True or false: Wycliff Jean attempted to become president of Haiti.

691) WHO WAS THE FIRST RAPPER TO HEADLINE THE GLASTONBURY MUSIC FESTIVAL?

    A) DR. DRE   B) EMINEM
    C) 50 CENT   D) JAY-Z

692) What rapper created

The Slim Shady LP?

● ●

693) In what year did Puff Daddy decide to be renamed P. Diddy?

a) 1995   b) 2001
c) 2003   d) 2005

● ● ● ● ● ● ● ● ● ● ● ●

LIVE

1st Time on stage together:

PUFF DADDY! AND **P. DIDDY!**

WITH OPENING ACT: **Diddy!**

694) Who did Jay-Z face off with in a 2001 notorious rapping battle?

a) Nas   b) Nose c) Nus   d) Nise

695) True or false: Dr. Dre was punched in the face as he was about to receive a Vibe Lifetime Achievement Award.

696) In 1990, a Florida record store owner was arrested over what 2 Live Crew album?
a) *Move Somethin'*   b) *As Nasty As They Wanna Be*
c) *Banned in the U.S.A.*   d) *The Real One*

697) When did Tupac Shakur die?
a) 1990   b) 1996   c) 1998   d) 2000

698) True or false: Coolio's "C U When U Get There" samples Pachelbel's "Canon in D."

699) Was *2pacalypse* Now released before or after Tupac Shakur's death?

700) Was *Still I Rise* released before or after Tupac Shakur's death?

701) Was *Me Against the World* released before or after Tupac Shakur's death?

702) Was *All Eyez on Me* released before or after Tupac Shakur's death?

703) WAS *LOYAL TO THE GAME* RELEASED BEFORE OR AFTER TUPAC SHAKUR'S DEATH?

704) True or false: There was a rapper named Lil' Scrappy.

705) **True or false:** There was a rapper named Dreddy Kruger.

706) True or false: There was a rapper named Marz Bar.

707) True or false: There was a rapper named Messy Marv.

708) True or false: Both Ludacris and Snoop Dogg are featured on Chingy's song "Holidae In."

709) Who is not featured on Drake's song "Forever"?
a) Kanye West
b) Lil Wayne
c) Eminem
d) Snoop Dogg

710) Who was featured on the Eminem hit "Love the Way You Lie"?
a) Rihanna
b) Dr. Dre
c) Missy Elliott
d) Mary J. Blige

****
711) What numeral is featured twice in the title of an MC Hammer hit?
****

712) Lil Wayne, Lil' Kim, or Lil Jon & The East Side Boyz: Who recorded "Yeah!"?

713) LIL WAYNE, LIL' KIM, OR LIL JON & THE EAST SIDE BOYZ: WHO RECORDED "IT'S ALL ABOUT THE BANJAMINS"?

* *

714) Lil Wayne, Lil' Kim, or Lil Jon & The East Side Boyz: Who recorded "Magic Stick"?

* *

715) Lil Wayne, Lil' Kim, or Lil Jon & The East Side Boyz: Who recorded "Down"?

716) Lil Wayne, Lil' Kim, or Lil Jon & The East Side Boyz: Who recorded "Lillipop"?

717) Lil Wayne, Lil' Kim, or Lil Jon & The East Side Boyz: Who recorded "Lovers & Friends"?

1) a
2) *Mary Poppins*
3) a 3, b 5, c 6, d 2, e 1, f 7, g 4
4) before
5) Blake Lively
6) a
7) b
8) true
9) true
10) true
11) a. *Won*, b. *River*, c. *Rider*, d. *Commandments*
12) a. *Desire*, b. *Ark*, c. *Dead*, d. *Din*
13) Steve
14) Greg—yellow shirt
15) true
16) *Happy Days* (255)
17) *X-Files* (202)
18) *Bewitched* (254)
19) *Will & Grace* (193)
20) *Star Trek: Deep Space Nine* (176)
21) true
22) false
23) true
24) false
25) true
26) true
27) Game Show Network
28) Spanish
29) Oprah Winfrey Network
30) American Movie Classics
31) Independent Film Channel
32) Country Music Television
33) b
34) b
35) true
36) true
37) Adult Swim
38) true
39) Video Hits
40) false
41) true
42) true
43) true
44) Barbra Streisand
45) *Dreamgirls*
46) eight
47) true
48) b
49) *Transformers: Revenge of the Fallen*
50) *Transformers: Dark of the Moon*
51) c
52) false—Illinois
53) d
54) false
55) b

56) two
57) the Riddler
58) black and white
59) George Clooney
60) Meryl Streep
61) b
62) a
63) a) *It Takes Two;*
    b) *Billboard Dad;*
    c) *Switching Goals;*
    d) *Passport to Paris;*
    e) *Our Lips Are Sealed*
64) d
65) false
66) true
67) false
68) true
69) false
70) *Teen Wolf*
71) *I Was a Teenage Frankenstein*
72) *Land Before Time*
73) *Godzilla*
74) *Nightmare on Elm Street*
75) c
76) a
77) c
78) 30 Rockefeller Plaza
79) *Saturday Night Live*
80) *Stargate SG1* (214)

81) *M*A*S*H*
82) *Married With Children* (259)
83) four
84) b
85) d
86) Comcast
87) c
88) true
89) Washington
90) Brooklyn
91) Montreal
92) false
93) c
94) Milwaukee
95) a 1, b 4, c, 2, d 3
96) d
97) a
98) Jackie Robinson
99) d
100) Casey Stengel
101) false—1986 Boston Red Sox also did this
102) true
103) a 1, b 5, c 7, d 2, e 8, f 3, g d, h 6
104) Peyton and Eli Manning
105) true
106) b
107) c
108) d

109) Al Davis
110) Joe Namath
111) false—no team has
112) a
113) Thelonious Monk
114) a 1, b 4, c 3, d 2
115) a
116) c
117) b
118) true
119) a 5, b 4, c 1, d 2,
     e 3, f 6
120) before
121) Milwaukee and Los
     Angeles
122) true
123) c
124) England
125) true
126) False—fields eleven
127) true
128) true—in 1998
129) no
130) forty-five
131) b
132) true
133) true
134) false—five minutes
135) true
136) six
137) true
138) nine
139) goaltender

140) three
141) "Rip Van Winkle"
142) Cassius Clay
143) a
144) true
145) true
146) Robinson
147) Ray Charles
148) Leonard
149) Jack Dempsey
150) false—it's named for
     an English town
     and school
151) five
152) two
153) three
154) d
155) d
156) d
157) broken
158) solid
159) solid
160) eight
161) yes
162) true
163) false
164) true
165) false—it goes back to
     1652
166) a
167) c
168) four
169) boat rod

170) c
171) false—the bigger the number the smaller the hook
172) d
173) c
174) carp float
175) mono line
176) surgeon's knot
177) shockleader knot
178) true
179) true
180) a
181) b
182) d
183) deepwater
184) d
185) b
186) true
187) true
188) c
189) false
190) no—but on very large plants
191) true
192) raisins
193) green beans
194) Eggplant
195) horseradish
196) lettuce
197) true
198) false
199) true

200) true
201) Michigan
202) a
203) true
204) hot dogs
205) a
206) true
207) b
208) Hardee's
209) false—it was founded by Glen Bell
210) Chihuahua
211) false—*Today Show* weatherman Willard Scott
212) false—it comes from the Raffel brothers, the original owners
213) BK Joe
214) d
215) b
216) false—only around 1,500
217) Thank Goodness It's
218) red and white
219) b
220) b
221) c
222) false
223) true
224) true
225) family
226) false

227) chicken planks
228) false
229) c
230) true—it's based in Atlanta
231) true
232) true
233) true
234) 1950s
235) true
236) true
237) false—although it is thought to help keep away evil spirits
238) true—It's in Middleton, Wisconsin
239) c
240) Bazooka
241) b
242) false—it's an urban legend
243) 100 Grand
244) a
245) Charleston Chew
246) true
247) Bit-o'-Honey
248) Twix
249) true
250) false—there's a Qu side
251) true
252) sixteen
253) sixteen
254) six and nine
255) you can move back one space
256) six
257) one
258) b
259) fifteen
260) four
261) true
262) false
263) six
264) three
265) one
266) four
267) true
268) c
269) card
270) ten
271) d
272) World War II
273) two
274) yes
275) d
276) d
277) eighteen
278) three
279) yes
280) yes
281) yes
282) Fs
283) Ds
284) c

285) a
286) b
287) no
288) no
289) yes
290) true
291) true
292) Colonel Mustard
293) true
294) a
295) false—Marvin Gardens, which is actually spelled Marven Gardens, is in nearby Margate City, NJ
296) more
297) true
298) true
299) false—it was worth $2 million
300) d
301) nine
302) no
303) seven
304) true
305) false—Charles Darrow was the inventor, and there's evidence that he copied an earlier game
306) true

307) he or she stays It along with the tagged person
308) a
309) false— it was just 30 hours
310) yes
311) in
312) balls
313) no
314) true
315) c
316) eight
317) curve, straight, slider
318) it's considered an out
319) d
320) nine
321) Germany
322) c
323) Africa
324) true
325) b
326) true
327) true
328) true
329) c
330) false
331) a
332) true

333) false—but there is one under Yellowstone National Park
334) c
335) c
336) d
337) Greenland
338) d
339) c
340) true
341) c
342) c
343) b
344) true
345) stream
346) creek
347) tributary
348) begin
349) right bank
350) a
351) yes
352) false
353) mouth
354) Blue Nile
355) White Nile
356) August
357) d
358) true
359) false
360) true
361) Minnesota
362) yes

363) d
364) Genoa
365) no
366) false—it was Hernando de Soto
367) true
368) true
369) false
370) Russia
371) China
372) Russia
373) true
374) true
375) Erie
376) Michigan
377) Superior and Huron
378) false
379) true
380) false—200
381) true
382) oxygen
383) a helicopter
384) false—he was 76 years old
385) K2
386) Mt. McKinley—but only by about 1,000 ft.
387) false—they are in South Carolina
388) d
389) true
390) the southeast

391) fault line
392) the epicenter
393) a
394) the aftermath
395) d
396) true
397) a
398) b
399) a
400) d
401) false
402) d
403) Jasmine
404) Mulan
405) Pocahontas
406) Cinderella
407) Ariel
408) c
409) false
410) Pocahontas
411) c
412) c
413) Belle
414) Ariel
415) Cinderella
416) Aurora
417) c
418) New Orleans
419) false
420) c
421) townspeople
422) b
423) b

424) a
425) a restaurant
426) Ray
427) a
428) false—but she is blind
429) true—she's Eudora, Tiana's mother
430) *Pinocchio*
431) *Sleeping Beauty*
432) *Lady and the Tramp*
433) *Alice in Wonderland*
434) *Dumbo*
435) *The Aristocats*
436) *Pete's Dragon*
437) *Aladdin*
438) *The Lion King*
439) *Hercules*
440) *Mulan*
441) *Enchanted*
442) *Lilo and Stitch*
443) *The Emperor's New Groove*
444) *Tarzan*
445) *Pocahontas*
446) *The Little Mermaid*
447) *Beauty and the Beast*
448) *101 Dalmatians*
449) *Peter Pan*
450) *Cinderella*
451) *Bambi*

452) *The Hunchback of Notre Dame*
453) *The Jungle Book*
454) *Snow White and the Seven Dwarfs*
455) false
456) c
457) true
458) Donald Duck
459) c
460) false—Hopper
461) scream
462) laugh
463) true
464) false
465) no
466) yes
467) false—Garrett only
468) yes
469) false
470) c
471) Elasti-girl
472) b
473) c
474) d
475) No
476) *A Bug's Life*
477) *Cars*
478) *Cars 2*
479) yes
480) d
481) d
482) yes
483) yes
484) yes
485) c
486) true
487) Woody
488) Pizza Planet
489) c
490) b
491) dog
492) true
493) false
494) false—it was his first
495) false—Hasbro wouldn't give permission for him to be used at all
496) d
497) d
498) c
499) c
500) false
501) Bullseye
502) true
503) c
504) Radiator Springs
505) b
506) b
507) true
508) a
509) false—Michael Caine
510) c
511) d

512) c
513) d
514) b
515) c
516) a
517) Larry the Cable Guy
518) *Mater's Tall Tales*
519) d
520) true
521) b
522) Johnny Cougar
523) Stacy Ferguson
524) a
525) Mark Twain
526) Elton John
527) a 5, b 1, c 3, d 4, e 6, f 2
528) false—William Claude
529) true
530) false—Orenthal James
531) true
532) true
533) Ron Artest
534) a
535) true
536) true
537) false—Bo Diddley
538) Cartoonist
539) rock musician
540) philosopher
541) Methodist minister
542) economist
543) mathematician
544) Guardian of Scotland
545) Mexican revolutionary leader
546) photographer
547) Prime minister of Japan
548) 20th-century American writer
549) founder of *Time*
550) mathematician
551) chairman of GE
552) commercial pitchman
553) yes
554) yes
555) no
556) no
557) true
558) false—Jane's niece, Peter's daughter
559) true
560) a 1, b 2, c 4, d 2
561) no
562) no
563) Natalie Wood
564) true
565) a 5, b 1, c 4, d 2, e 3
566) Rolling Stones
567) John Lennon
568) Stevie Wonder

569) R.E.M.
570) Van Morrison
571) c
572) a
573) Fleetwood Mac
574) Prince
575) Queen
576) c
577) Bruce Springsteen
578) TLC
579) Goo Goo Dolls
580) The Police
581) ABBA
582) Van Halen
583) 'N Sync
584) b
585) The Go-Go's
586) Billy Joel
587) Madonna
588) Elton John
589) Cyndi Lauper
590) Eminem
591) true
592) after
593) true
594) no
595) no
596) no
597) (Time of Your Life)
598) (Everything I Do)
599) (Forget About Me)
600) toward the source of the music

601) a
602) d
603) true
604) false—there's an intro section that begins "While the storm clouds gather far across the sea..."
605) Philadelphia Flyers
606) a
607) b
608) a
609) true—George M. Cohan
610) true
611) true
612) false
613) false—but she did write the lyrics
614) true
615) c—although she was teaching summer classes at Colorado College
616) true
617) c
618) before
619) b
620) c
621) b
622) true—*Born on the Fourth of July*
623) true

624) b
625) a
626) a
627) b
628) c
629) *The College Dropout*
630) b
631) a
632) true
633) Coolio
634) false—but it was used in the film
635) b
636) true
637) true
638) false—the title of Zevon's song was "Werewolves of London"
639) true
640) a
641) true
642) false
643) Kanye West
644) seventeen
645) false—just *Alice in Wonderland*
646) true
647) true
648) true
649) Tim McGraw
650) true
651) a 3, b 2, c 5, d 1, e 4

652) a 4, b 1, c 2, d 5, e 3
653) Aretha Franklin
654) U2
655) The Eagles
656) The Backstreet Boys
657) The Supremes
658) The Rutles
659) *A Mighty Wind*
660) Spinal Tap
661) d
662) c
663) true
664) true
665) "that golden valley"
666) true
667) false
668) true
669) b
670) b
671) true
672) true
673) a, c, and e
674) true—Enrico Caruso singing "Vesti la Giubba"
675) Ludwig van Beethoven
676) Wolfgang Amadeus Mozart—and, actually, Antonio Salieri
677) a
678) Animals

679) a
680) *Fantasia*
681) *1812 Overture*
682) the Lone Ranger
683) four
684) d
685) a
686) A funeral mass
687) a
688) b
689) true
690) true
691) d
692) Eminem
693) b
694) a
695) true
696) b
697) b
698) true
699) before
700) after
701) before
702) before
703) after
704) true
705) true
706) false
707) true
708) true
709) d
710) a

711) 2—in the song "2 Legit 2 Quit"
712) Lil Jon & The East Side Boyz
713) Lil' Kim
714) Lil' Kim
715) Lil Wayne
716) Lil Wayne
717) Lil Jon & The East Side Boyz

About Applesauce Press

GOOD IDEAS RIPEN WITH TIME. FROM SEED TO HARVEST,
APPLESAUCE PRESS CREATES BOOKS WITH BEAUTIFUL
DESIGNS, CREATIVE FORMATS, AND KID-FRIENDLY INFORMATION.
LIKE OUR PARENT COMPANY, CIDER MILL PRESS
BOOK PUBLISHERS, OUR PRESS BEARS FRUIT TWICE A YEAR,
PUBLISHING A NEW CROP OF TITLES EACH SPRING AND FALL.

"WHERE GOOD BOOKS ARE READY FOR PRESS"
VISIT US ON THE WEB AT
WWW.CIDERMILLPRESS.COM
OR WRITE TO US AT
12 PORT FARM ROAD
KENNEBUNKPORT, MAINE 04046